Cambridge Elements

Elements in Shakespeare Performance
edited by
W. B. Worthen
Barnard College

SHAKESPEARE AND THE RESTORATION REPERTORY

Stephen Watkins
University of Greenwich

CAMBRIDGE
UNIVERSITY PRESS

Shaftesbury Road, Cambridge CB2 8EA, United Kingdom

One Liberty Plaza, 20th Floor, New York, NY 10006, USA

477 Williamstown Road, Port Melbourne, VIC 3207, Australia

314–321, 3rd Floor, Plot 3, Splendor Forum, Jasola District Centre,
New Delhi – 110025, India

103 Penang Road, #05–06/07, Visioncrest Commercial, Singapore 238467

Cambridge University Press is part of Cambridge University Press & Assessment,
a department of the University of Cambridge.

We share the University's mission to contribute to society through the pursuit
of education, learning and research at the highest international levels of excellence.

www.cambridge.org
Information on this title: www.cambridge.org/9781009324137

DOI: 10.1017/9781009324120

© Stephen Watkins 2025

This publication is in copyright. Subject to statutory exception and to the provisions
of relevant collective licensing agreements, no reproduction of any part may take place
without the written permission of Cambridge University Press & Assessment.

When citing this work, please include a reference to the DOI 10.1017/9781009324120

First published 2025

A catalogue record for this publication is available from the British Library

ISBN 978-1-009-32413-7 Paperback
ISSN 2516-0117 (online)
ISSN 2516-0109 (print)

Cambridge University Press & Assessment has no responsibility for the persistence
or accuracy of URLs for external or third-party internet websites referred to in this
publication and does not guarantee that any content on such websites is, or will
remain, accurate or appropriate.

Shakespeare and the Restoration Repertory

Elements in Shakespeare Performance

DOI: 10.1017/9781009324120
First published online: March 2025

Stephen Watkins
University of Greenwich

Author for correspondence: Stephen Watkins, s.watkins@greenwich.ac.uk

ABSTRACT: This Element provides the first comprehensive study of William Davenant's Shakespeare adaptations within the broader context of the Restoration repertory. Moving beyond scholarship that tends to isolate Restoration Shakespeare from the other plays produced alongside it, this Element reveals how Davenant adapted the plays in direct response to the institutional and commercial imperatives of the newly established theatre industry of the 1660s. Prompted by recent developments in early modern repertory studies, this Element reads Restoration Shakespeare as part of an active repertory of both old and new plays through which Davenant sought to realize a distinctive 'house style' for the Duke's Company. Finally, it shows how Restoration Shakespeare was mobilized as a key weapon in the intense competition between the two patent theatres until Davenant's death in 1668.

KEYWORDS: Shakespeare, William Davenant, Restoration theatre, adaptation, repertory

© Stephen Watkins 2025

ISBNs: 9781009324137 (PB), 9781009324120 (OC)
ISSNs: 2516-0117 (online), 2516-0109 (print)

Contents

1	Introduction	1
2	Establishing Actors' 'Lines'	15
3	LIF House Style	33
4	Supernatural Rivals	48
5	Continuity and Innovation	63
6	Conclusion	78
	References	83

1 Introduction

When the theatres reopened following the restoration of the Stuart monarchy in 1660, one of the most pressing issues that they faced related to repertory. The absence of professional playing since 1642 meant that there were few, if any, active playwrights working in London who could be called upon to produce new scripts on demand, and in the scramble to establish viable enterprises there was considerable tussling over what were known as the 'Old Stock Plays' (Downes 1987, p. 24) – the pre-war texts that could be dusted down and presented afresh to audiences (Sorelius 1965; Hume 1981).[1] The very earliest months of the decade saw a number of different groups attempt to establish a foothold in the new industry. John Rhodes (*fl.* 1624–65), for example, assembled a company of young, inexperienced actors, including Thomas Betterton (1635–1710), who moved into the Cockpit on Drury Lane, the site of several licensed performances of operatic entertainments, complete with painted perspective scenes, in the 1650s (Watkins 2019); the veteran King's Men actor Michael Mohun (1616?–84) organized a troupe of older actors at the Red Bull theatre; while the theatre proprietor and manager William Beeston (1606?–82) anticipated the King's return in 1659 (and thus the return of the theatre) by arranging repairs to Salisbury Court, the theatre he had run back in the 1630s (Hotson 1928, pp. 82–132; Freehafer 1965). Eventually, though, two men emerged as the sole beneficiaries of the new regime, handpicking actors and, for the first time, actresses from these more amorphous groupings to create their own companies. Thomas Killigrew (1612–83) and William Davenant (1606–68) were granted patents by King Charles II that effectively bestowed upon them a theatrical duopoly that subsisted (barring a period in the 1680s when they merged into the United Company) until the nineteenth century. Between them, Killigrew's King's Company and Davenant's Duke's Company – named for its patron, James, Duke of York – dominated the theatre industry in the 1660s, driving out all other

---

[1] Of the professional playwrights who had written dramas before 1660, only James Shirley, Thomas Killigrew, and William Davenant were still alive; none of them wrote any new original plays after the Restoration.

competition (Hume 2004; Payne 2024; Watkins forthcoming). Having set the scene for their own success, they now needed to secure rights to the old stock plays and begin performing for audiences.

This was more complicated than it initially appeared. As the manager of the King's Company, which consisted mainly of older actors who were original King's Men from before the war – actors like Mohun, Theophilus Bird (1608–63), Walter Clun (d. 1664), and Charles Hart (1625–83) – Killigrew felt entitled to claim the plays produced by the pre-war company as his property. This included of course all of Shakespeare's plays as well as the majority of plays from the likes of Beaumont and Fletcher, Ben Jonson, Thomas Middleton, John Webster, and Philip Massinger. It even included many of Davenant's own plays written during the Caroline period, which represented a real problem for the Duke's Company manager – he could not even rely on his own back catalogue of scripts to furnish his new enterprise. We do not know exactly what the rationale was for dividing up the old stock plays, but, after much pleading with the Lord Chamberlain, a compromise was reached and Davenant was eventually granted access to his own works as well as nine Shakespeare titles: *Hamlet*, *Henry VIII*, *King Lear*, *Macbeth*, *Measure for Measure*, *Much Ado About Nothing*, *Romeo and Juliet*, *The Tempest*, and *Twelfth Night* (Hume 1981, pp. 158–159). He also picked up other important texts, like Webster's *Duchess of Malfi*. With both companies now in possession of a set of producible scripts, they began performing, training up their actors, building an audience, and commissioning new writers to compose new works that could supplement the old as quickly as possible.

As Amanda Eubanks Winkler and Richard Schoch (2022, p. 73) acknowledge in their recent book on Davenant, 'it remains beyond doubt that the Duke's Company was seriously disadvantaged from the outset in terms of the range and variety of dramatic works that it could produce'. Certainly, Killigrew's company retained the rights to the vast majority of pre-war texts, and Davenant's plays amounted to a paltry number in comparison. To compensate, Davenant relied on theatrical innovation. In June 1661, he moved into his new theatre at Lincoln's Inn Fields (hereafter LIF). This had been converted from a tennis court and was now equipped with a system of wing-and-shutter scenes; this meant that he could stage plays with painted perspective scenery that changed between scenes to represent a number of different locations. Davenant had been a pioneer of this technology, which he had imported from the continent during the 1650s in productions of his first through-composed opera, *The Siege of Rhodes*, staged initially at his private residence, Rutland House, in 1656 before transferring to the Cockpit in 1658 (Southern 1952; Lewcock 2008; Watkins 2019). Indeed, Davenant chose to open his new theatre in 1661 with *Rhodes*, this time presenting it as a spoken play rather than an opera (Davenant 1973). This kind of technology represented for English audiences a sensational and revolutionary transformation from pre-war practice. While it was perfectly feasible to produce pre-1642 repertory with scenes, Davenant desperately wanted to present plays that were specifically designed to showcase this new asset to best advantage (Hume 2004, pp. 54–55). Killigrew, on the other hand, had in 1660 moved his actors into a theatre on Vere Street. This was also converted from an earlier tennis court – Gibbon's – but boasted no scenic technology of any kind. Instead, it resembled much more closely the kinds of Jacobean indoor theatres like the Blackfriars, with their naked stages, with which his older company had been familiar before the wars (Leacroft 1973; Langhans 1982; Keenan 2017). While the King's Company could not entice audiences with the latest in theatrical technology, then, they nevertheless produced a wide range of shows to engage a performance-hungry audience – these were experienced actors working with known scripts on more-or-less familiar terrain. If he wanted seriously to compete with the King's Company, Davenant had to level the field of play by devising productions that could show off what his theatre and its company were really capable of.

These were the institutional and material circumstances that precipitated the Shakespeare adaptations for which Davenant became notorious.[2] From this, we can see that 'Shakespeare held the predominant place' (Eubanks Winkler and Schoch 2022, p. 73) in the LIF repertory. He had to, by necessity: Davenant did not have the luxury of selecting from a wide range of old stock scripts as Killigrew did. He could not afford to be

---

[2] See Summers, ed., 1922; Spencer 1927; Harbage 1935; Edmond 1987; Dobson 1992; Murray 2001; Eubanks Winkler and Schoch 2022.

picky. Over the course of five years, between 1662 and 1667, Davenant produced four outright adaptations: *The Law Against Lovers* (1662), which grafted the Beatrice and Benedick plot from *Much Ado About Nothing* onto the Isabella and Angelo narrative from *Measure for Measure*; *The Rivals* (1664), a reworking of Shakespeare and Fletcher's *The Two Noble Kinsmen*; *Macbeth*, which provided elaborate musical episodes for the witches and enhanced the character of Lady Macduff; and, in collaboration with John Dryden, *The Tempest, or the Enchanted Island* (1667), which gave Miranda and Caliban sisters (Dorinda and Sycorax respectively), as well as a love interest for Dorinda, Hippolito. During the same period, he staged performances of the other Shakespeare plays in his possession in either unaltered or in heavily cut forms. *Henry VIII*, as we shall see, was performed as originally written but with lavish scenes that proved extremely popular; *Twelfth Night* was likewise revived as written but received only isolated performances in the early years of the company; *Romeo and Juliet* may have been produced in both its original form and an adaptation by John Crowne (Spencer 1965–66). Most famously, Davenant produced a heavily cut version of *Hamlet* for performance in 1661, which would become one of Thomas Betterton's most celebrated roles. Back in 1927, Hazelton Spencer made the case that the 1676 edition of that play represented Davenant's performance text. The printed edition contains a 'Note to the Reader', which states that, '*THis Play being too long to be conveniently Acted, such places as might be least prejudicial to the Plot or Sense, are left out upon the Stage: but that we may no way wrong the incomparable Author, are here inserted according to the Original Copy with this Mark*' (Shakespeare 1676, sig. [A2 r]). While *Hamlet* is not an adaptation as such, it was nevertheless 'ruthlessly cut' (Spencer 1927, p. 176) by Davenant in such a way as to alter the overall balance between the actors' parts in ways that reveal much about his approach to the production. However, because *Hamlet* displays very limited evidence of responding directly to the wider repertory, I have refrained from extensive comment on it in what follows.

Restoration Shakespeare scholarship to date has tended to discuss Davenant's adaptations as discreet entities, isolating them from the larger group of plays – both old stock *and* new – that Davenant deliberately curated in order to compete commercially with his rival, Killigrew. Indeed, while there has been a consistent and growing interest in Restoration Shakespeare in recent decades, it is conspicuous that critics all too frequently neglect to attend to the repertory contexts in which it was produced. For an earlier generation of scholars, for example, it was enough simply to compare how the adaptations by the likes of Davenant, Dryden, and Nahum Tate (*King Lear* [1681]) matched up to their source texts. Invariably, these critics found the Restoration versions wanting, deploring the ways in which their adaptors sacrificed the sublime poetry and psychological complexity supposedly inherent in Shakespeare in favour of insipid (modernized) language and meaningless spectacle. The nineteenth-century editor of the Variorum *Tempest*, Horace Howard Furness (1892, p. viii), for example, wrote of Davenant and Dryden's version that 'No imagination, derived from a mere description, can adequately depict its monstrosity, – to be fully hated it must be fully seen'. Spencer, writing in *Shakespeare Improved* (1927, p. 203), concurred: 'Gone is the noble serenity that makes us eager to regard *The Tempest* as Shakespeare's farewell message to the world; in its place we have a licentious farce. Everything that the authors lay their hands on is defiled.'

More recent commentators (on the whole) have moved away from such hostile invective and have instead tried to take the texts on their own literary and dramaturgical terms. This kind of criticism covers three broad and often overlapping areas: textual and verbal differences between an adaptation and its source text; the politics of authorship and politico-ideological critique; and the conditions of performance, especially in relation to music and spectacle. In *Restoration Shakespeare: Viewing the Voice* (2001), for example, Barbara A. Murray charts the divergences between the source play and its adapted version on textual grounds, arguing that the adaptations resulted from a desire on the part of Restoration playwrights to 'make his [Shakespeare's] language operate more like speaking pictures' (p. 32). This approach has the virtue of seeing the new works as worthy of study in their own right, but Murray tends to enumerate the verbal alterations made by the adaptors while ignoring material factors such as casting and costume that might also inform how a play was adjusted in the period. Others have been more successful in illuminating the adaptations on literary-critical grounds, opening up their engagement with contemporary (i.e. Carolean) politics. Michael Dobson (1992), Nancy Klein Maguire (1992), Susan J. Owen (2002), and Emma Depledge (2018), for example, all read the adaptations as coded responses to the peculiar political circumstances of the Restoration and its aftermath in the Exclusion Crisis and Popish Plot (*c*.1678–82). In these accounts, Shakespeare's rise to cultural prominence, to use Depledge's phrase, is a direct result of the ways in which Restoration playwrights reworked the plays to comment on potentially incendiary topics. Venting their ideas through the lens of Shakespeare rather than through an original work, Restoration theatre makers and adaptors could fall back on what Annabel Patterson (1984, p. 18) terms 'functional ambiguity' should the authorities take offence at what was being staged. These studies have revealed precisely how Restoration playwrights mobilized Shakespeare's texts to broach controversial ideas while telling us something important about changing notions of authorship – and bardolatry – in the later seventeenth century.

Finally, in the last decade or so another area of study has begun to preoccupy scholars interested in Restoration Shakespeare. This relates to the practical questions of how these texts might have been performed in the period and, as an extension, how we might go about restaging them meaningfully for audiences today. Prompted by exponents of Practice-as-Research (PAR) in Shakespeare and early modern theatre studies, scholars such as Tim Keenan (2009), Tiffany Stern,[3] Sara Reimers (2023), and others have used performance methodologies to explore what kinds of challenges and opportunities these scripts offer to actors in performance. Most significantly, between 2017 and 2019, Amanda Eubanks Winkler and Richard Schoch, along with their Research Fellow, Claude Fretz, brought together actors, early music specialists, and theatre scholars to investigate how plays like Davenant's *Macbeth* (1664) and Thomas Shadwell's expanded operatic version of the Davenant-Dryden *Tempest* (1674) worked on stage, given their demanding technological requirements (including flying machines and

---

[3] In 2015, Stern worked with the Texas-based theatre company, the Hidden Room, on an historically informed production of Tate's *King Lear* (1681). The production is available to view at <https://vimeo.com/452882823> [accessed 12 November 2024].

trapdoors), their extensive use of music and dance, and their new characters and plot scenarios. Under the aegis of their project, 'Performing Restoration Shakespeare', which was funded by the UK's Arts and Humanities Research Council, they collaborated with Shakespeare's Globe Theatre in London and the Folger Theatre in Washington, DC, to explore how these adaptations might be realized on stage. The project culminated in a professional production of Davenant's *Macbeth*, directed by Robert Richmond with music direction by Robert Eisenstein at the Folger Theatre in September 2018 (Payne 2017; Reimers and Schoch 2019). I had the extreme good fortune to be invited along to the Folger, along with six other scholars, to advise on rehearsals and to discuss Davenant's text with the actors and musicians. (The other scholar-consultants were Sarah Ledwidge, Lisa A. Freeman, Deborah C. Payne, Sara Reimers, and Andrew R. Walkling.) I also contributed a chapter on Davenant's *Macbeth* to a collection of essays deriving from our time on the project (see Eubanks Winkler, Fretz, and Schoch 2023).

The opportunity to test out our ideas about Davenant's adaptations in a PAR context transformed our thinking about Restoration Shakespeare texts in performance, enabling us to take them seriously as works of theatre, demonstrating beyond doubt that they are compelling dramatic vehicles, even if – or especially when – they depart radically from their Shakespearean parent texts. In their book-length study, *Shakespeare in the Theatre: Sir William Davenant and the Duke's Company* (2022), which resulted from their work on the project, Eubanks Winkler and Schoch provide us with a detailed historical and practical account of the kinds of performance issues that attend Restoration Shakespeare, ranging from how actors were trained and rehearsed to their use of gesture, vocal technique (e.g. singing), and stage movement. Devoting special attention to Davenant's most musically complex adaptations, *Macbeth* and *The Tempest*, Eubanks Winkler and Schoch (2022, p. 3) mount a compelling argument for approaching Restoration Shakespeare 'as a complex theatrical – indeed, intermedial – experience and not merely as a dramatic text, let alone a dramatic text presumed inferior to its precursor'.

This Element seeks to contribute to this growing body of scholarship on Davenant's adaptations in particular and Restoration Shakespeare more generally by asking how and why Davenant altered his scripts in the ways that he did. It argues that in order to answer those questions fully we need to place Shakespeare's works – both in unaltered *and* altered forms – within the wider repertory of which they made up a substantial part. This contention is predicated on the belief that the Restoration theatre was, in the end, an actor's theatre rather than a writer's one, and that plays only reached the stage if management was confident their performers could make a success of them. In his survey of Restoration drama, Robert D. Hume (1976, p. 22) emphasized the necessity of placing plays within their theatrical contexts in order to fully gauge their significance:

> Reading a play here and a play there, and very probably not even knowing which house put it on, we get a very inadequate sense of the circumstances in which late seventeenth-century drama flourished. Experienced writers almost invariably wrote specifically for one company or the other; consequently, they knew precisely what actors would be available and for what sort of roles. When one house did well, the other might try to steal its thunder [. . .] by imitation, or produce a novelty as a counter-attraction, or mock the success.

Davenant, like every playwright in the period, wrote with particular actors in mind, and his knowledge of their talents and skills would have informed how he approached his Shakespearean scripts. By comparing which actors played which parts in the adaptations with their other roles in the same season (when we have evidence for these), we can build a picture of how Davenant envisaged his adaptations working in performance. Indeed, as the company manager, Davenant oversaw casting decisions for every production; as such, he could use his adaptations to push an actor in a particular direction or type of role. He might offer an opportunity for a minor actor to step into a leading part or punish a leading one for some slight (real or perceived) by demoting them to a bit-part. Thus, examining Davenant's adaptations within the context of LIF's broader repertory has the potential to reveal how far inter-personal relationships developed and changed across the 1660s between actors and management.

The approach to Restoration Shakespeare adopted in this Element has been influenced by recent studies of the early modern theatre repertory by, among others, Roslyn L. Knutson (1991), Scott McMillin and Sally-Beth MacLean (1998), and Tom Rutter (2017). Early modern repertory studies offer Restoration theatre historians a useful line of attack because they focus on contextualizing surviving play-texts within a 'company-oriented' (Rutter 2017, p. 4) paradigm. The emphasis here is on how a particular play came to signify within the repertorial logics of a particular company (or across companies), and what this might tell us about the ways a company constituted its sense of identity. In their study of the Queen's Men repertory, for example, McMillin and MacLean (1998, p. xii) argue that through their decision making about personnel, acting style, staging methods, verification, and repertory, playing companies developed 'special characteristics' that came to be peculiarly associated with them. This helped to foster a sense of shared corporate identity among company members even as it enabled the company to distinguish itself clearly from its competitors in an increasingly crowded marketplace. As McMillin and MacLean (1998, p. xii) summarize: 'organizations within a profession always develop identities of their own, widely recognized features which stand out from the procedures they share with other organizations'. This corporate identity in turn went on to determine the kinds of plays that a company prioritized for inclusion in their repertory – they needed to maintain a recognizable and distinctive style (or brand) in order to encourage potential patrons to spend their disposable incomes with them rather than their competitors – and this began to affect the kinds of work playwrights produced. Eventually, these 'special characteristics' developed into a 'house style'. Tom Rutter (2017) builds on this notion of a company house style in his study of the 'evolving and reciprocal relationship' between the Lord Chamberlain's Men and their rivals, the Admiral's Men. His investigation into the development of their respective repertories shows that playwrights working for the opposing companies nevertheless 'drew on each other's work' (p. 6) even as they adjusted their plays to accommodate the 'distinctive qualities' (p. 12) of their particular playhouse. In his analysis, Rutter shifts 'the focus from the dramatist to the playing company' to better reflect 'the priorities of early modern theatrical culture, which did not privilege playwrights over players as modern criticism often has'; instead, his company-oriented approach 'opens up space for the discussion of practices that originated as much, or more, in the company as in the playwright, such as acting style, staging and repertory management' (p. 12).

Shakespeare and the Restoration Repertory thus aims to contribute to our understanding of Davenant's adaptations by showing how they responded to other plays – both new and 'Old Stock' – that were already present in the Duke's Company's repertory as well as in that of their rival, the King's Company. Doing so will enable us better to understand how the intense commercial rivalry between Davenant and Killigrew in the 1660s determined how the repertory came to look in these years, and especially how the pressures of economic competition affected the ways Davenant adjusted Shakespeare's texts. As well as telling us something about LIF's internal company dynamics, then, a repertory approach to Restoration Shakespeare also sheds light on a major scholarly contention of the period: the nature of the competition between the two patent theatres. Hume (2004, p. 54) insists that '[t]he importance of competition to the writing and staging of new plays can hardly be overemphasized. When two companies competed vigorously, quite a lot of new plays got staged each year.' This was certainly the case, as Riki Miyoshi's survey (2012) of the plays produced by both companies during the years 1663–8 demonstrates. However, while there has been a considerable and concerted effort to take a repertory approach to the Restoration theatre in recent years, this has thus far failed to account adequately for how individual plays responded to commercial imperatives on the micro-level of script development. While we know that Davenant and Killigrew were in fierce competition in, say, 1663–4, no one has yet explored how that competition impacted the repertory of that particular season directly. Instead, Restoration repertory studies, as traditionally practiced, either survey the establishment and growth of dramatic genres in general (using heuristics dissociated from commercial-industrial factors) or they concentrate on the day-to-day management, economics, and rivalrous squabbles between managements (leaving the plays themselves behind).[4] Despite the attention theatre historians of the Restoration period have paid to the material circumstances, economic structures, and management infrastructure of the two patent companies, remarkably little systematic analysis has been conducted on their respective repertories as distinct but mutually constituting phenomena, although Deborah C. Payne's recent *Business of English Restoration Theatre, 1660–1700* (2024) does provide us with a new and compelling model.[5] To date, no one has seriously explored the question of whether Killigrew or Davenant were consciously manufacturing a distinctive house style in a way analogous to the pre-1642 companies investigated by McMillin and MacLean and Rutter. One of the aims of this Element, then, is to address the question of company house style in relation to LIF's repertory, which includes Davenant's Shakespeare adaptations. In doing so, we will more accurately discern how the competition between the Duke's Company and the King's Company operated. We will see that, rather than both companies seeking to put the other out of business, with Davenant frequently leading the attack, the rivalry was more good-natured and balanced than this. At certain moments, Killigrew held the advantage in terms of popularity or prestige, and Davenant was forced to adapt his practices to compensate.

This Element is structured in five sections that each address how Davenant's adaptations of Shakespeare responded to, and were informed by, on the one hand internal company issues (e.g. actor availability), and on the other, inter-company competition (e.g. popular new plays at the other theatre). In Section 2, I argue that Davenant's amalgamation of two Shakespeare scripts – *Much Ado About Nothing* and *Measure for Measure* – into *The Law Against Lovers* must be seen in direct relation to his very first production at LIF, *The Siege of Rhodes*. Despite the 'dire need for new plays on the part of the Duke's Company' (Hume 2004, p. 5), for his first new production after *Rhodes*, Davenant decided to conflate two of his hard-won

---

[4] For examples of the first approach, see Rothstein 1967; Hume 1976; Rothstein and Kavenik 1988; for the second, see Milhous 1979; Miyoshi 2012.

[5] Payne's book appeared too late for me to incorporate its rich and compelling arguments fully into my text, but I acknowledge it here as an important advance on our understanding of this topic.

old stock scripts into a single play. What would be the motivation for doing so if he merely wanted to fill the maximum number of performance slots with the minimum of effort? I suggest that he elected to do so in order to provide his young and inexperienced company of actors with a performance text that clearly built on their previous success with *Rhodes*. *Rhodes* had opened LIF in June 1661 (*LS*, p. 29) to great success, according to the long-standing prompter at LIF, John Downes (1987, p. 51), who produced a history of the of the Duke's Company in 1708: 'All Parts being Justly and Excellently Perform'd; it continu'd Acting 12 Days without Interruption with great Applause'. Originally staged as a through-sung opera in 1656, *Rhodes* was now performed as a spoken play, albeit retaining significant amounts of music.[6] An early prototype of the rhymed heroic drama that would come to dominate the repertories of both playhouses later in the decade, *Rhodes* presents audiences with a compelling love-and-honour plot based on Suleiman I's siege of the island of Rhodes back in 1522 (Davenant's major source was Richard Knolles's *The General History of the Turks*, the fourth edition of which was printed in 1631). The plot revolves around the cross-cultural conflict and resolution between the Muslim Ottomans and the Christian Rhodians and the visiting Italians, Alphonso and Ianthe, who are newly married. Caught in the crossfire, Ianthe goes to Solyman to beg for safe passage for her and her husband, only for Solyman to proposition her; she remains virtuous and Solyman, struck by her goodness, repents. Alphonso, however, is prompted to jealously by the encounter and fights on behalf of the Rhodian forces. This is the *locus classicus* of the heroic drama's private honour versus public duty motif (Waith 1971, pp. 194–198). Moreover, the play utilizes an elaborate musical and visual semiotics that sets out a model for the kinds of scenic plays Davenant's company would produce in its earliest seasons.

By modelling *The Law Against Lovers* on the only other 'new' play so far staged at LIF, Davenant offered his actors an opportunity to consolidate

---

[6] In a famous account of the Restoration heroic play, Dryden (1956–2002, vol. 9, p. 9) claimed that Davenant 'was forc'd' to turn *Rhodes* into an opera to circumvent the prohibition on stage plays during the 1650s – a view later endorsed by Dent (1928), p. 66: 'it seems highly probable that D'Avenant originally wrote

and develop their respective 'lines' within the company; that is, with playing a character of a similar type to their earlier role in *Rhodes*. Davenant's first Shakespeare adaptation consciously drew on the heroic motifs and love-and-honour themes of *Rhodes*, and this suggests a reason for collapsing two scripts into one at such an early stage in the company's life. Davenant was only too aware of the need to build on his actors' limited experience, and so he slowly introduced new works into the repertory at steady intervals, providing them with parts analogous to those they had already mastered in earlier productions, thus ensuring consistently competent performances from each member of his company. Rather than searching for political or aesthetic reasons for why Davenant wrote *Law Against Lovers* as he did, I argue that we need to see it as part of a training season, in which he exposes each of his actors to the types of characters they would specialize in going forward.

Section 3 then considers the emergence of a putative house style at LIF. It considers the plays produced between 1663 and 1665, when the competition between the two patent companies began in earnest. The 1663–4 season, in particular, was challenging for Davenant commercially. Not only had his rival now moved into a scenic theatre – Bridges Street – meaning that the King's Company could mount plays full of scenic spectacle, but Davenant's authority within his own company was being undermined from within. One of his leading actors, Henry Harris, was unhappy with his position within the company, and with the kinds of parts he was playing, and threatened to defect to the other playhouse. Overcoming these difficulties in a financially advantageous way meant consolidating a production style that, on the one hand, was sufficiently different to Killigrew's and, on the other, that could find a space to accommodate Harris, who had been angling for better (and more remunerative) parts. To resolve these two problems in one move, Davenant staged Shakespeare's *Henry VIII* in a lavish production that showed off to

the work as a drama in rhymed heroic couplets, and that it was only when he found it impossible to produce it as a play, that he decided to turn it into an opera'. More recent scholarship, however, has shown that Davenant always intended *Rhodes* to be through-sung. See Walkling 2017 and Watkins 2019.

best advantage the kind of visual and musical spectacle available at LIF, while offering Harris the chance to play the dramatically captivating role of Cardinal Wolsey opposite the most celebrated actor of the period, Thomas Betterton as Henry VIII. This play would serve as a prototype for LIF house style: a beautifully decorated and carefully rehearsed history play, complete with a love triangle, which enabled Harris to rival Betterton in both dramatic arc and audience affection. *Henry VIII* would set the bar for subsequent plays. It included accurate costuming and scenery, authentic music, and elaborately choreographed stage movements, including dance interludes. As we will see, Davenant followed this up with newly commissioned plays by hot young writers like Roger Boyle, earl of Orrery, which followed the same model but which further incorporated rhyme (now synonymous with heroic drama) into the mix. In the next season, Davenant built on these two productions with *The Rivals*, yet again placing an inordinate value on scenic verisimilitude, impressive costuming, and cleverly incorporated music and dance.

Section 4 then addresses Davenant's landmark production of *Macbeth* in November 1664. Having established LIF house style, I argue that this production was developed in direct response to commercially and critically celebrated plays at the other playhouse. Prior to 1664, Davenant had never staged a play that included elements of the supernatural. Indeed, he had in fact developed a rather sophisticated philosophical rationale for dismissing such things. But the success of a supernatural play at Killigrew's theatre earlier in the year prompted Davenant to reassess his commitment to verisimilar drama and instead produce *Macbeth*, complete with its singing and dancing witches. This section shows – contrary to most scholarship that sees Davenant as always leading the way in terms of theatrical innovation – that this was a moment when he was actually caught out by Killigrew's creative ambitions. *Macbeth* was an attempt to compensate for his negligence and cash in on a new form of theatre that was causing a sensation with audiences at the rival playhouse.

In Section 5, I turn away from the ways in which *Macbeth* differs from established LIF house style to consider how it simultaneously built on those established company practices and traditions. In particular, I reassess what we know about the original casting of *Macbeth* to suggest that Davenant, while consciously adjusting his praxis to counter Killigrew, remained committed to promoting particular 'lines' for his actors in his plays. The section concludes with an analysis of *The Tempest*, considering that play in the light of Betterton's prolonged absence from the stage during the 1667–8 season due to illness, asking how this opened up new opportunities for other actors to come to the fore. In particular, it situates the play within a vogue for cross-dressed characters and youthful casts to argue that Davenant, now working with Dryden, specifically adapted the play to showcase the young actresses of the company; by comparing the play with Sir George Etherege's *She Would If She Could* (1668), which similarly included no part for Betterton, we can gain a sense of exactly what Davenant's priorities were for his company during this season. Finally, the Conclusion draws out some of the continuities across the period as a whole in the ways Shakespeare was situated within the broader Restoration repertory and makes the case for taking the wider view when it comes to exploring the ways plays are analysed from this period.

By placing Davenant's adaptations of Shakespeare from this period within the context of the broader repertory that surround them, we can begin to erode longstanding commonplaces about Restoration theatre in general and about Davenant's theatrical aesthetics in particular. The standard narrative holds that Davenant was the consummate man of the theatre, always leading the way in terms of innovation and commercial appeal, while the ineffectual and incompetent Killigrew lagged, incompetently, behind. But this obscures a much messier and more volatile picture. By exploring the ways in which Davenant adapted Shakespeare in the 1660s in response to the wider repertory – both that of his own theatre and that of his rival's – this Element reveals how economic opportunism, corporate identity (or, at the very least, brand recognition), changes in personnel, and commercial rivalries all played a central role in the ways Davenant developed his scripts for performance.

2 Establishing Actors' 'Lines'

Law Against Lovers was the first 'new' play written specifically with the members of Davenant's Duke's Company in mind. Prior to its premiere on 15 February 1662, Davenant appears only to have staged performances of pre-1660 plays (*LS*, pp. 29–47). Of these, *The Wits* (1634) and *Love and Honour* (1633) were his own works, while *The Cutter of Coleman Street* (1661) was by his old friend, the poet Abraham Cowley, who had recently been given a one half-share in the company for 'Assistance & Judgment in Writing Correcting & providing Tragedies Comedies And other Poetic Entertainments for the stage' (quoted in Hotson 1928, p. 221). (*Cutter* was in fact a revision of Cowley's 1641 play, *The Guardian*, and was completed sometime before the Restoration, likely in 1658, when the play is set.) The rest were unaltered texts by Shakespeare, Massinger, and Fletcher (one with Rowley): *Hamlet* (c.1601), *Twelfth Night* (1602), *The Bondman* (1623), *The Mad Lover* (c.1617), and *The Maid in the Mill* (c.1623). Where these works were produced more-or-less as originally written or, as in the case of *Hamlet*, with significant cuts, *Law Against Lovers* represented a significant departure in repertory policy. It was a labour-intensive enterprise: Davenant carefully grafted the Benedick-Beatrice love-plot from *Much Ado About Nothing* onto the main action of *Measure for Measure*. To ensure a dramatically satisfying outcome, he had to compose entirely new scenes and introduce newly invented characters, including Beatrice's little sister Viola. He incorporated new song and dance interludes, appealing to theatrical fashions and audience expectations, and he made hundreds of smaller verbal adjustments to Shakespeare's texts in order to effect a major overhaul of the moral and psychological structures of the play.

Given the paucity of extant plays available to the Duke's Company in these early seasons, we might hesitate to ask why Davenant would expend precious time and energy on turning two perfectly viable performance vehicles (Shakespeare's original works) into just one (untried) production; as Katherine Scheil (2003, p. 29) asks, surely he 'would want to get as much mileage out of each play that he was allowed to stage' as possible, rather than carving up and sacrificing ready-made material? Earlier commentators have explained Davenant's decision to merge his Shakespearean sources with reference to the ideological imperatives and scenic spectacle typical of the heroic dramas that were popular in the period (Rothstein and Kavenik 1988, pp. 6–40; Kroll 2007, following Harbage 1935 and Gellert 1979). For Nancy Klein Maguire (1992, pp. 63–64) and Michael Dobson (1992, pp. 33–36), for instance, Davenant remodelled the play to conform to the

Fletcherian tragicomedies that dominated the stage in these early seasons, such as Sir William Killigrew's *Selindra* (1662), which offered audiences moral commentaries on the recent political upheavals of the 1640s and 1650s. Scheil (2003, p. 30) argues that, given his role as theatre manager, Davenant 'was intensely conscious of the need to create a successful play, and this imperative took precedence over any desire to create political parallels or correct Shakespeare'. The addition of musical interludes and scenic spectacle is, for Scheil, a direct attempt to provide the kinds of novelty expected by Restoration audiences.

It is certainly the case that Davenant sought to model *Law Against Lovers* on the Fletcherian tragicomedies that were entering the repertory at this time and that were driven by a desire to increase the musical-spectacular theatrics on display at LIF. But these accounts do not fully explain why Davenant chose to collapse two easily producible plays into one: the Angelo-Isabella plot alone has sufficient political parallels to contemporary politics (sexually corrupt Puritans were standard Restoration fare), and both of Shakespeare's texts could easily accommodate musical expansion. To answer that question, we need to consider issues of casting and repertory in the 1661–2 and 1662–3 seasons. Davenant's was a relatively young and inexperienced company in 1662, and he needed to provide his actors, essentially, with training texts through which they could hone their stage skills and develop audience awareness of their individual talents. As a result, *Law Against Lovers* was written with a view to further developing each actors' particular 'line' within the genre of the Fletcherian tragicomic play. Only by transplanting the Beatrice-Benedick plot to *Measure for Measure*'s central narrative, along with the extra characters he added to this storyline, did Davenant create a play with enough parts for his core company (there are eighteen speaking parts of varying sizes, including five for women). This process had begun with *Rhodes* the previous year; that play thus served as a working model when Davenant came to adapt his first Shakespeare. What part an actor successfully played in *Rhodes* (and other pre-1660 plays) would likely determine any future roles written specifically for them.

As Peter Holland (1979, pp. 77–78) and Tiffany Stern (2000, pp. 152–153) have shown, actors in the Restoration period cultivated particular 'lines' or 'casts' – that is, stereotyped characters – that they tended to play across the repertory: kings, rakes, fops, clowns, villains, lovers, and so on. This typecasting not only enabled actors to 'memorise hundreds of parts and be able to act them with minimal re-rehearsal' (Holland 1979, p. 77), but it also meant that audiences came to expect a certain kind of performance from them irrespective of the specific text they were playing. When Samuel Sandford, famed for his portrayal of villain roles, attempted to play 'an honest man' in one performance *c.*1690, for example, the audience 'fairly damned it, as if the author had imposed upon them the most frontless or incredible absurdity' (Cibber 2022, p. 97). We can see Davenant adapting *Law Against Lovers* on the basis of the character types and plot scenarios offered up works like *The Siege of Rhodes*. In both plays, a young, virtuous woman (Ianthe in *Rhodes*; Isabella in *Law Against Lovers*) pleads with a usurping authority figure (Solyman; Angelo) for the release from captivity of her family member (Alphonso; Claudio). That authority figure is initially presented to the audience as morally suspect and corrupt, with sexual undertones, only to be finally vindicated as entirely honourable. Angelo, we learn in Act 4 of *Law Against Lovers*, was only ever testing Isabella's virtue; he never actually risks sexual violence against her, nor does he intend to carry out the death penalty on Claudio, as he does in Shakespeare. Instead, he is represented as just, fully intending to marry Isabella from the start. In a late exchange, he reveals that he has merely been testing her resolve throughout:

> *Ang.* Forgive me who, till now, thought I should find
> Too many of your beauteous Sex too kind.
> I strove, as jealous Lovers curious grow,
> Vainly to learn, what I was loth to know.
> And of your virtue I was doubtful grown,
> As men judge womens frailties by their own.
> But since you fully have endur'd the test,
> And are not only good, but prove the best
> Of all your Sex, submissively I woo
> To be your Lover, and your Husband too.
> (Davenant 1673, p. 315; second pagination)

In similar vein, in the second part of *Rhodes*, Solyman the Magnificent tries his wife Roxolana's fidelity and obedience by insinuating an affair with Ianthe. At that play's close, however, he reveals 'In this I have your [Roxolana's] virtue try'd' (Davenant 1973, 5.6.177), before freeing his captives in a generous act of mercy.

No cast-list survives for *Law Against Lovers*, but it is possible to conjecture who in Davenant's company took which role, given what we know about the other casting choices Davenant made for his actors during the 1661–2 and 1662–3 seasons.[7] Table 1 sets out which actor likely played which part, identifying the particular 'line' the character belongs to, as well as all the other named roles we know they played between 1662 and 1664. I also signal any specific characteristics or talents (physicality, musical talents, proficiency in dancing, etc.) that the script of *Law Against Lovers* calls for. Finally, I pair the character from *Law Against Lovers* with its equivalent role in *The Siege of Rhodes* in order to suggest how Davenant built his Shakespeare adaptation on the foundations of the earlier production. This is not to say, however, that the equivalent parts were necessarily played by the same performer (in some cases, as the Table makes clear, this is not possible), but it shows how Davenant was thinking in terms of character types and lines when he altered his source texts.

We can see from this list how *Law Against Lovers* was most likely cast in the 1661–2 season, and thus how the play was understood to conform to the emerging 'lines' of each actor. It is very likely, for example, that Betterton played Angelo, given that he is presented, as Gellert (1979) and Harbage (1935, p. 257) both assert, as a flawed heroic lover in Davenant's version, akin to Solyman the Magnificent in *Rhodes*. Angelo is initially presented to the audience as a disruptive and potentially dishonourable figure in his attempted seduction of Isabella (his initial intention to marry her is only revealed to us late in the play), but he is ultimately shown to be 'an essentially honourable figure' (Gellert 1979, p. 31). He is also the senior

---

[7] For establishing actors' 'lines' across the Restoration repertory, I have found Juan A. Prieto-Pablos's database, 'Restoration Actors and Actresses and their Acting Roles', Universidad de Sevilla, indispensable: <https://institucional.us.es/restorationactors/web/> [accessed 12 November 2024].

Table 1 Conjectural cast-list for *Law Against Lovers*, c. 1662

Character in Law against Lovers	Line/Distinctive Attributes	Actor at LIF in 1662	Equivalent 'line' in *The Siege of Rhodes*	Subsequent Roles in the Heroic and Shakespearean Repertory, 1661–64
Duke of Savoy	Governors, Dukes, Kings, Old Men	Thomas Lilliston	Villerius, Grand Master of Rhodes	Claudius (*Hamlet*) Duke of Savoy (*Love and Honour*) Dorvile (*The Villain*) Suffolk (*Henry VIII*) Canterbury (*Henry the Fifth*)
Lord Angelo, Deputy of Turin	Lead Heroes, Redeemable Usurpers, Misanthropes	Thomas Betterton	Solyman the Magnificent	Elder Palatine (*The Wits*) Hamlet (*Hamlet*) Sir Toby Belch (*Twelfth Night*) Alvaro (*Love and Honour*) Bondman (*The Bondman*) Jolly (*Cutter of Coleman Street*) Mercutio (*Romeo and Juliet*) Bosola (*Duchess of Malfi*) Brisac (*The Villain*) Don Henrique (*Adventure of Five Hours*) Iberio (*The Slighted Maid*)

			Filamor (*The Step-Mother*)
			King Henry (*Henry VIII*)
			Beauford (*The Comical Revenge*)
			Owen Tudor (*Henry the Fifth*)
			Philander (*The Rivals*)
	Romantic Heroes, Just Ruler, Heirs (second to Betterton) Singer	Henry Harris	Younger Palatine (*The Wits*)
			Horatio (*Hamlet*)
			Sir Andrew Aguecheek (*Twelfth Night*)
			Prospero (*Love and Honour*)
			Young Trueman (*Cutter of Coleman Street*)
Benedick, brother to Angelo[a]		Alphonso, a Cicilian Duke	Romeo (*Romeo and Juliet*)
			Ferdinand (*Duchess of Malfi*)
			Beaupré (*The Villain*)
			Antonio (*Adventures of Five Hours*)
			Salerno (*The Slighted Maid*)
			Wolsey (*Henry VIII*)
			Frollick (*The Comical Revenge*)
			King Henry (*Henry the Fifth*)
			Theocles (*The Rivals*)

[a] Spelled '*Benedict*' in 'The Names of the Persons' (Davenant 1673, p. 272; second pagination), but '*Benedick*' throughout the play.

Table 1 (Cont.)

Character in Law against Lovers	Line/Distinctive Attributes	Actor at LIF in 1662	Equivalent 'line' in *The Siege of Rhodes*	Subsequent Roles in the Heroic and Shakespearean Repertory, 1661–64
Lucio	Loyal Companions to Lead Character	William Smith	Mustapha, Bassa?	Antonio (*Duchess of Malfi*) Corrigidor (*Adventures of Five Hours*) Lugo (*The Slighted Maid*) Crispus (*The Step-Mother*) Buckingham (*Henry VIII*) Bruce (*The Comical Revenge*) Burgundy (*Henry the Fifth*) Polynices (*The Rivals*)
Balthazar	Loyal Companions	Robert Nokes	Rustan, Bassa?	Gioseppe (*The Slighted Maid*) Sergius (*The Step-Mother*) Exeter (*Henry the Fifth*)
Eschalus, a Counsellor	Old Councillors, Comic Boobies	Thomas Lovel	Admiral of Rhodes?[b]	Polonius (*Hamlet*) Malvolio (*Twelfth Night*) Old Trueman (*Cutter of Coleman Street*) Gracchus (*The Step-Mother*)

[b] Apparently taken by Nicholas Blagden (*fl.*1660–68), who transferred to the King's Company in December 1661, and was thus not available for *Law Against Lovers* (*BD*, vol. 2, p. 143; Milhous and Hume 1991, #119).

Character	Role Type	Actor	Other Role	Examples
Claudio, in love with Julia	Lovers, Loyal Servants, Companions	Joseph Price	Pirrhus, Vizier Bassa	Guildenstern (*Hamlet*) Leonel (*Love and Honour*) Will (*Cutter of Coleman Street*) Paris (*Romeo and Juliet*) Maleteste (*Duchess of Malfi*) Colignii (*The Villain*) Silvio (*Adventures in Five Hours*) Fromund (*The Step-Mother*) Sandys (*Henry VIII*) Dufoy (*The Comical Revenge*)
Provost	Villains, Machiavels, Servants (esp. Prison wardens)	Samuel Sandford	High Marshal of Rhodes?	Worme (*Cutter of Coleman Street*) Sampson (*Romeo & Juliet*) Maligni (*The Villain*) Ernesto (*Adventures of Five Hours*) Vindex (*The Slighted Maid*) Sylvanus (*The Step-Mother*) Wheadle (*The Comical Revenge*) Arras (*Henry the Fifth*) Provost (*The Rivals*)
Fryar Thomas	Old Men, Friars	John Richards	N/A	Ghost (*Hamlet*) Friar (*Romeo and Juliet*) Castruccio (*Duchess of Malfi*)

Table 1 (Cont.)

Character in Law against Lovers	Line/Distinctive Attributes	Actor at LIF in 1662	Equivalent 'line' in *The Siege of Rhodes*	Subsequent Roles in the Heroic and Shakespearean Repertory, 1661–64
Bernardine, a Prisoner		?	Attendant to Roxolana?[c]	
Jaylor	Clown/Comedian, Grotesques, Humorous companions, servants Unattractive face: "This fellow looks like a man boy'ld | In pump-water (Davenant 1673, p. 301; second pagination); "Tis impudence to show so bad a face | In good company' (Davenant 1673, p. 308)[d]	Cave Underhill		Sir Morglay Twack (*The Wits*) First Gravedigger (*Hamlet*) Feste (*Twelfth Night*) Cutter (*Cutter of Coleman Street*) Gregory (*Romeo and Juliet*) Diego (*Adventures of Five Hours*) Peralta (*The Slighted Maid*) Tetrick (*The Step-Mother*) Winchester (*Henry VIII*) Palmer (*The Comical Revenge*) Bedford (*Henry the Fifth*) Cunopes, the Provost's Man (*The Rivals*)

[c] Q1663 of *Rhodes* lists 'Four Pages' as attendants to Roxolana.
[d] Cf. with descriptions of Underhill's ugly face and physical appearance in *BD*, vol. 15, p. 84.

Fool/Under-Jaylor	Singer Comedians, Servants, Bit-parts	James Nokes or Mr Dacres	Haly, Eunuch Bassa?[e]	Nokes: Puny (*Cutter of Coleman Street*) Nurse (*Romeo and Juliet*) Menanthe (*The Slighted Maid*) Norfolk (*Henry VIII*) Sir Nicholas Cully (*The Comical Revenge*) Constable of France (*Henry the Fifth*) Dacres: Second Gravedigger (*Hamlet*) Soaker (*Cutter of Coleman Street*)
Beatrice, a great Heiress	Lead Female Roles, esp. Virtuous Heroines, Witty Lovers, Queens and Rulers	Mary Betterton (née Saunderson)	Iantha, wife to Alphonso	Ophelia (*Hamlet*) Melora (*Love and Honour*) Cleora (*The Bondman*) Aurelia (*Cutter of Coleman Street*) Juliet (*Romeo and Juliet*)

[e] John Downes played this part at the opening of LIF, but the sight of playing before the '*August* presence' of the king and his entourage, he tells us, 'spoil'd me for an Actor', and so he ceased acting and become the company's prompter instead (Downes 1987, p. 73).

Table 1 (Cont.)

Character in Law against Lovers	Line/Distinctive Attributes	Actor at LIF in 1662	Equivalent 'line' in *The Siege of Rhodes*	Subsequent Roles in the Heroic and Shakespearean Repertory, 1661–64
	'She is yet very exceedingly virtuous [...] but, Sir, she has too much wit, and great wits will not long lye idle' (pp. 282–83) Singer (occasional)			Duchess (*Duchess of Malfi*) Belmont (*The Villain*) Porcia (*Adventures of Five Hours*) Pyramena (*The Slighted Maid*) Caesarina (*The Step-Mother*) Queen Katharine (*Henry VIII*) Graciana (*The Comical Revenge*) Princess Katherine (*Henry the Fifth*) Heraclia (*The Rivals*)[f]
Isabella, Sister to Claudio	Virtuous Heroines, Sexually Complicated Women, Loyal Servants	Anne Gibbs Shadwell	Roxolana, wife of Solyman[†]	Gertrude (*Hamlet*)[†] Olivia (*Twelfth Night*)[†] Evandra (*Love and Honour*)[†] Lucia (*Cutter of Coleman Street*) Julia (*Duchess of Malfi*) Ericina (*The Slighted Maid*)

[f] Mary Betterton played Heraclia in the original run of *The Rivals* in 1664, but the cast-list in Q1668 names Anne Gibbs (Shadwell) in the role (see below).

[†] Played by Hester Davenport prior to her departure from the company in February 1662; Gibbs Shadwell appears to have inherited most of her parts, except Roxolana, who, according to Downes (1987, p. 26), Mary Betterton took over at some point (although he perhaps confuses *The Siege of Rhodes* for its sequel, *Mustapha*, in which Betterton certainly did play Roxolana).

Julietta, Mistress to Claudio	Bit part player, eps. Companions and Maids	Jane Long	Melosile, Attendant to Ianthe?	Jane (*Cutter of Coleman Street*) Flora (*Adventure of Five Hours*) Diacelia (*The Slighted Maid*) Brianella (*The Step-Mother*) Mrs Rich (*The Comical Revenge*) Queen of France (*Henry the Fifth*) Leucippe (*The Rivals*)
Viola, Sister to Beatrice; very young[g]	Bit part player, esp. Companions and Maids 'very young' (cast-list for *Law Against Lovers*); 'Small Mistress' (p. 275) Singer Dancer Instrumentalist (castanets/guitar)	Moll Davis	Madina Attendant to Ianthe?	Violinda (*The Step-Mother*) Aurelia (*The Comical Revenge*) Princess Anne (*Henry the Fifth*) Celania (*The Rivals*)

[g] Pepys (1995, vol. 3, p. 32) mentions a 'Little Girle' singing and dancing.

Table 1 (Cont.)

Character in Law against Lovers	Line/Distinctive Attributes	Actor at LIF in 1662	Equivalent 'line' in *The Siege of Rhodes*	Subsequent Roles in the Heroic and Shakespearean Repertory, 1661–64
Francisca, a Nun	Older Women, esp. Widows, Wives, Nuns	Mrs. Holden or Peg Fryer	Attendant to Roxolana?	Holden: Paris's wife (Crown's *Romeo and Juliet*) Fryer: Old Widow (*Love and Honour*)?[h]

[h] See *LS*, p. 4l.

ranking character – the elder brother of Benedick – and thus would be reserved for the senior actor in the company, reflecting Betterton and Harris's respective positions at this time within the company. Betterton tended to play older or more high-ranking characters to Harris's younger lovers, rakes, and companions: the Elder Palatine to Harris's Younger Palatine in *The Wits*; Sir Toby Belch to Sir Andrew Aguecheek in *Twelfth Night*; Hamlet to Horatio, and so on. Betterton also appears to be exploring misanthropic and world-weary parts at this time: Hamlet and Bosola, for instance, reflect some of Angelo's ennui at the state of the world through their extensive soliloquies. At the other end of his career, moreover, Betterton would reprise the role of Angelo in Charles Gildon's adaptation of *Measure for Measure*, *Beauty the Best Advocate* (1699), where again illicit sexuality is avoided by having Angelo clandestinely marry Mariana. With Betterton cast in the role, Angelo would be understood in the early scenes at least as a very real political and sexual threat; his powers lay in his ability to show the transition from erotic passion to heroic noblesse by the play's end.

Harris would have been the natural choice to play Benedick, given his developing line in romantic leads. That line began with Alphonso in *Rhodes* and took in such characters as Theocles in *The Rivals* and Romeo in *Romeo and Juliet*. Harris was a good-looking and confident young actor and would go on to specialize in comic-romantic leads, often in partnership with one of the company's leading actresses, such as Mary Betterton (née Saunderson) or Anne Gibbs (later Shadwell). A talented singer as well as actor and scene painter, he was frequently called upon to sing in duet or choruses in performance. Benedick is no exception: in Act 5, scene 1, he has a trio with Beatrice and her young sister, Viola (Davenant 1673, p. 317; second pagination).

The minor male roles all have equivalent parts in *Rhodes*, even if it is not always entirely clear who would have played which part. Thomas Lilliston was known for his governor roles – he played Villerius, the Grand Master of Rhodes, in *Rhodes*, as well as Claudius in *Hamlet*, for example – and would surely have played the Duke who leaves Angelo in charge of Savoy at the beginning of the play, while Lovel, a noted Polonius and Malvolio, would probably have played Eschalus, the old and rather tedious counsellor. Sandford seems to have made a good line in Provosts, and Cave Underhill, the Company's leading comedian, would be the obvious choice for the Jaylor, assisted by another of the company's comedians as the Under-Jaylor, given the repeated references to his unattractive facial features, for which he was famous. The Fryar Thomas was likely the responsibility of John Richards, who would also play the Friar in *Romeo and Juliet*. Other roles would have been taken by hirelings on an ad hoc basis (*LS*, p. lvii).

It is more difficult to discern which female parts in the play most clearly fit the lines of individual actresses in this period. This is partly because there were abrupt changes in the roster of actresses available at the Duke's Company over these months. We are probably safe to hypothesize that Mary Betterton played Beatrice, given that she regularly played witty romantic leads alongside Harris in tragicomedies, comedies, and heroic plays of this period: she was Ianthe to Harris's Alphonso in *Rhodes*, for example, and would go on to play the Juliet to his Romeo later in the season. (So associated was she with the role of Ianthe in Pepys's mind that this became her sobriquet in his diary.) Evidently, she could be relied upon to turn on a sixpence between youthful innocence and emotional distress: in addition to Ianthe and Beatrice, she was also selected as Ophelia in the Duke's Company's *Hamlet* and likely played Melora in *Love and Honour*, who ends up marrying Betterton's Alvaro. Again, this suggests that she was selected for *Law Against Lovers* for her ability to switch between comic brio and emotional poignancy, as when she tests Benedick's loyalty: 'Would I might trust you *Benedick*' (Davenant 1673, p. 293; second pagination). Although not particularly known as a strong singer like Harris or Moll Davis, Mary Betterton was clearly able to carry a tune: if the 1676 quarto of *Hamlet* reflects Restoration performance practice, she was called upon to provide 'remnants of old lauds' (Shakespeare 1676, p. 72) as Ophelia in Act 4, scene 1, and Davenant called on her vocal resources again in the Act 5 trio in *Law Against Lovers* mentioned earlier.

The central role of Isabella was likely intended for Hester Davenport, who was until late 1661 or early 1662 Davenant's leading actress. She played opposite Thomas Betterton in nearly all the plays they performed together in the opening season. She was Lady Ample, the witty match to Betterton's Elder Palatine, in *The Wits*; she took the role of Evandra in *Love and Honour*, and she played Gertrude in *Hamlet* – the largest female part in a very male-dominated play. She became particularly famous for her performance as Roxalana, Solyman's domineering but ultimately virtuous wife, in *Rhodes*; both Pepys and Evelyn refer to her in their diaries as 'Roxolana'. Isabella would thus have provided her with an especially strong, independent, and virtuous character to work with, and it certainly would appear that Davenant adapted the play with her in mind for the part. However, Davenport left acting to become mistress to the Earl of Oxford sometime before performances of *Law Against Lovers* began: the play premiered on 15 February and Pepys (1995, vol. 3, p. 32) lamented her absence from the company when he saw it three days later (see also Downes 1987, p. 74). Her hasty departure meant that her parts had to be quickly redistributed among the remaining actresses, and it would appear that Anne Gibbs took on the bulk of her roles, including Gertrude in *Hamlet*. Gibbs was herself a celebrated actress who was clearly cultivating a line in virtuous and chaste heroines all her own: she had played the mournful but strong-willed Olivia in *Twelfth Night*, and, as I will argue in Section 5, she probably originated the role of the hyper-moral Lady Macduff in *Macbeth* in 1664. Back in July 1661, some months before she joined Davenant's company, Gibbs seems to have played with the Red Bull company in Oxford, possibly with Davenport herself (Rosenfeld 1943, p. 366). (Anthony Wood [1891, p. 406] suggests that 'Roxilana' was present at these performances, which took place between 3 and 13 July 1661, but Pepys and Downes both place Davenport at LIF until at least 11 July, when the *Rhodes* first run is taken to have finished.) During her time in Oxford, Gibbs became particularly celebrated for her performances as Lucrecia in Thomas Heywood's *The Rape of Lucrece* (1608). So successful was she in this part that she inspired John Walden, a student at Queen's College, to write a series of poems in her honour. *Io Ruminans: or, the Repercussion of a Triumph Celebrated in the Palace of Diana Ardenna* (1662) was dedicated to the 'MOST HEROICALLY VIRTUOUS Mrs *Anne Gibbs*', whom he described as the '*Auxesis* of woman-kind' (sig. A3r and p. 10). Given her previous experience, she would have been an obvious choice to take over from Davenport the part of the chaste Isabella.

Finally, the smaller female parts were unsurprisingly taken by the younger and less experienced members of the company. Viola, for instance, was played by Mary (Moll) Davis (*fl.* 1660–98), a noted singer, dancer, and musician. She appears to have joined Davenant's company from its inception in 1661, but it might be that *Law Against Lovers* was her stage debut. Pepys (1995, vol. 3, p. 32) comments on the performance he saw on 18 February: 'saw *The Law Against Lovers*, a good play and well performed, especially the Little Girle's (who I never saw act before) dancing and singing'. Davis was certainly a juvenile when she began acting onstage. In *The Law Against Lovers*, she played Viola, who is noted in the cast-list as 'Sister to *Beatrice*; very young' (Davenant 1673, p. 272; second pagination). While relatively small, as we might expect for a novice, the part does demand some musical skill. Not only does Davis sing a solo early in the play ('*Wake all the dead!*'), but she also demonstrates her broader musical talent, at one point '*dancing a saraband awhile with castanietos*' (p. 304; second pagination). Davis was an accomplished instrumentalist as well as singer and dancer – she also played the guitar – something that Restoration adaptors of Shakespeare exploited. I would surmise that Jane Long played Julietta, another minor role; she tended to play bit-parts in these early seasons – particularly maids and companions – and Julietta, despite being Claudio's lover in the play, in fact, appears very little on stage; she is more talked about than an active performance vehicle. (I discuss Long's career more fully in Section 5.)

While my suggestions for casting *Law Against Lovers* must remain highly conjectural – and ultimately unprovable – my point is less concerned with associating particular actors with particular roles than it is with suggesting that Davenant adapted the play with the stock characters of its surrounding repertory in mind. *Law Against Lovers* does not echo *Rhodes* in every detail (Isabella and Beatrice do not directly correspond to Ianthe and Roxolana, for example), but it certainly does share its basic building blocks with this kind of heroic/tragicomic drama: governor, usurping figure who seeks to take charge, romantic hero and heroine, virtuous and selfless woman. This tells us something about Davenant's approach to his repertory and his actors' developing 'lines', and thus prompts us to consider why Shakespeare's plays were adapted in the ways they were during the opening decade of the Restoration. Davenant's motivations for adapting did not solely boil down to indiscriminately adding in musical and scenic spectacle or making the play reflect the politics of its Restoration moment; rather, he also sought a way of enabling his actors to hone their craft by providing them with a performance vehicle that worked within the logics and structures of the wider repertory to which they contributed. In the end, then, Davenant's approach to Shakespeare adaptation tells us something about the emerging house style at LIF in the decade following the reintroduction of the theatre.

3 LIF House Style

In his first two seasons Davenant produced a number of Shakespeare plays, but he only embarked on one major adaptation with *Law Against Lovers*, as we have seen. That play was intended to contribute to the number of rhymed (or semi-rhymed) tragicomedies that were quickly becoming a staple of the company's offerings, and it served to develop the actors' individual lines following on from the success of *The Siege of Rhodes*. For some months thereafter, the Duke's Company mounted only one-off performances of original Shakespeare works, suggesting they did not particularly chime with audiences: *Romeo and Juliet* on 1 March 1662 – 'the worst that ever I heard in my life' (Pepys 1995, vol. 3, p. 39); *Twelfth Night* on 6 January 1663 – 'a silly play' (Pepys 1995, vol. 4, p. 6); and *Hamlet*, possibly on 9 March (*LS*, p. 63) but certainly on 28 May 1663 (Pepys 1995, vol. 4, p. 162). Only new plays by Thomas Porter (*The Villain*) and Samuel Tuke (*The Adventure of Five Hours*)[8]

---

[8] *Adventures*, based on *Los empeños de seis horas* (printed 1657) by Antonio Coello (1611–52), is described on its title-page as 'A Tragi-Comedy', and as Hume (1976, pp. 73–74) avers, it contains many of the hallmarks that link it with *Law Against Lovers*: 'Its serious tone, love and honour dilemmas, and occasional couplet passages may seem to take the play a long way toward heroic drama. However, the entirely domestic setting and concerns, amusing servants, the lack of rant, and the romantic-comedy structure with double wedding in prospect at the end greatly

seem to have secured the kinds of extended first runs that indicated popularity with audiences (*LS*, pp. 56–61). When Davenant finally returned to adapting Shakespeare for the stage in 1663–4, the conditions under which he produced it were dramatically different. As Robert D. Hume (1976, p. 238) has observed, before the 1662–3 season, both companies were preoccupied with consolidating their duopoly and so concentrated on internal company matters, such as training actors, casting, and securing rights to old stock plays. Having done so, they could now begin to turn their attention outwards, to address what their competitors were up to. As a result, the commercial competition between the Duke's and King's companies intensified between 1663 and Davenant's death in 1668. Both managers began to commission many new plays (including adaptations) in response to box office hits at the other house in order to profit from them. At the same time, however, we can see both companies working hard to develop distinctive house styles that enabled spectators to distinguish between their respective offerings. These factors had a profound impact on the ways Shakespeare's plays appeared in the subsequent repertory.

Before examining these Shakespeare adaptations in depth, it will be useful to sketch out some of the pertinent material and institutional conditions under which they were produced, as there were a number of factors that determined the nature and intensity of the competition between Killigrew and Davenant from this season on. The competition began in earnest in May 1663, when the King's Company moved to their new playhouse in Bridges Street. This was a significant improvement on their previous residence. Vere Street had been hastily converted from Gibbon's Tennis court into a theatre in 1660 and was decidedly 'no thrills': it comprised an auditorium and a bare apron stage and had no capacity for scenic technology or for machine effects (Langhans 1980, p. 37). It was, in effect, a theatre for a by-gone age. As such, Killigrew, despite owning the rights to most of the pre-1642 repertory, could not compete with Davenant in terms of scenic display. This was about to change with his new playhouse. Bridges Street opened on 7 May with a production of Fletcher's *The Humorous Lieutenant*; Pepys (1995, vol. 4, p. 128) tells us that 'This day the new Theatre Royal begins to act *with scenes*' (my emphasis). Overnight, therefore,

limit the resemblance to heroic plays to come.' This could serve perfectly well as a description of Davenant's adaptation.

Davenant lost his distinctive edge; given their ability to produce plays with both actresses *and* scenes, the King's Company now represented a very real challenge to their rival's box office.

Scholarship has tended to dismiss Killigrew's competence as a theatre manager, typically advancing the view that Davenant was always the innovator with Killigrew persistently in reactionary mode. The story goes that, despite his problems with securing repertory and his reliance on a young and untried company of actors, Davenant quickly found a formula for success, based in part on his investment in scenic and musical spectacle. Judith Milhous's assessment (1979, p. 15) is typical: 'A survey of the interaction between the two companies during the remainder of Davenant's lifetime shows a very simple pattern. Davenant led and Killigrew followed. The circumstances demanded exactly what Davenant's inclinations led him to anyway – innovation.'[9] However, there have been more recent attempts to reassess Killigrew's management style, which show that he was, in fact, a more competent and engaged theatre professional (albeit inconsistently so) than is usually acknowledged. Riki Miyoshi (2012) and David Roberts (2013) have both provided compelling reinterpretations of the evidence to argue that Killigrew fought hard to establish a viable theatre enterprise and overtake his competitor by investing in new technologies and new theatre genres (such as foreign opera). The new Theatre Royal was central to this project.

Killigrew may well then have presented a real threat to Davenant's venture, and this bears on our discussion of Shakespeare in the Restoration repertory. The move to Bridges Street significantly levelled the field of play between the two companies: Killigrew could now entice audiences with the kinds of visual and musical splendour that had previously only been the preserve of the Duke's Company. In fact, it appears that Killigrew's new theatre even outclassed Davenant's in some key respects. Analysis of stage directions from plays from both theatres by Tim Keenan (2017) and Andrew R. Walkling (2019) has shown that while LIF utilized the wing-and-shutter system established by Davenant and John Webb in the 1650s to slide scenes

---

[9] This view of the competition between the two managers still dominates mainstream scholarship, which focuses disproportionately on Davenant. See, inter alia, Edmonds 1987; Lewcock 2008; Keenan 2017; Eubanks Winkler and Schoch 2022.

across the stage on grooves, it lacked other kinds of stage machinery such as cloud and wave machines and (possibly) rope-pullies (see also Southern 1952; Leacroft 1973, pp. 65–88). Bridges Street, on the other hand, incorporated the latest in these stage devices – it could, for example, fly actors across the stage on ropes, either individually or in pairs, and it could raise whole troupes of actors or musicians from under the stage to the ceiling. As Walkling (2019, p. 61) summarizes, while Bridges Street 'sported impressive changeable scenery on a par with that at Lincoln's Inn Fields', it went much further, boasting 'the kind of advanced machine technology that was not in evidence at the other house'. For the first time since the establishment of the duopoly, then – *pace* Milhous – Davenant trailed behind his rival in terms of theatrical innovation.

Two months after the opening of Bridges Street, another issue compounded Davenant's problems, this time coming from within his own ranks. The Duke's Company's second leading actor, Henry Harris, began agitating for more money and for better parts and threatened to defect to Killigrew's Company, in direct contravention of the terms of the royal patents granted in 1662 and 1663 (Milhous 1979, p. 4). Pepys (1995, vol. 4, p. 239) related the situation on 22 July 1663 via a gossipy conversation with his shoemaker, William Wotton. According to Wotton, Harris

> grew very proud and demanded *20l* for himself extraordinary there, [more] then Batterton or anybody else, upon every new play, and *10l* upon every Revive – which, with other things, Sir W. Davenant would not give him; and so he swore he would never act there more – in expectation of being received in the other House [. . .] He tells me that the fellow grew very proud of late, the King and everybody else crying him up so high, and that above Baterton, he being a more ayery man, as he is endeed.

Wotton is surely exaggerating the amounts demanded by Harris for individual new and revived plays; a typical actor-sharer could expect to earn between £45 and £150 *per annum*, so £20 for every new play would be astronomical (Payne 2024, p. 227). Nevertheless, Harris's newfound fame and celebrity had evidently gone to his head. The actor refused to perform until his demands were met, causing 'a great loss to the House'. The company appears to have made a show of proceeding without him, mounting a couple of productions over the vacation period and early into the new season: they put on Davenant's medley of one-act pieces, *Playhouse to be Let*, in August, before mounting a production of Robert Stapylton's *The Step-Mother* sometime in early October (*LS*, pp. 67 and 71); the printed edition makes a reference to the '*long Vacation*' (1664 sig. A3v), suggesting it was performed sometime after the start of Michaelmas Term on 9 October 1663. Harris is conspicuously absent from that play's cast-list. Both these plays required significant scenic and musical resources that would have competed with Bridges Street. For instance, Acts 3 and 4 of *Playhouse to be Let* were versions of *The History of Sir Francis Drake* (1659) and *The Cruelty of the Spaniards in Peru* (1658), both of which were originally staged at the Cockpit theatre as standalone entertainments in the late 1650s. *The Step-Mother* (like *Drake*) called for 'the operatic elements of recitative singing, scenic spectacle, and theatrical dancing to instrumental music' (Walkling 2017, pp. 196–197). But Davenant's troupe was clearly struggling in the absence of such a significant player. According to Pepys, the manager suspected that Killigrew was somehow funding Harris's strike to create maximum disruption to his rival's enterprise: Wotton intimates that the actor was being paid 'a stipend from the other House privately'.[10] In the end, Harris was finally placated and agreed to return to acting some four months after the initial *contretemps*. Pepys (1995, vol. 4, p. 347) noted in an entry for 24 October that, 'by the Duke of Yorkes persuasion, Harris is come again to Sir W. Davenant upon his terms that he demanded, which will make him very high and proud'. It took the direct intervention of the company's patron, the Duke of York, to negotiate terms acceptable to both parties. Harris was to be offered the minor court position of Yeoman of the

---

[10] Again, this could just be overenthusiastic gossip. David Roberts and Richard Palmer (forthcoming) have recently uncovered evidence that Harris removed himself to Bath in the summer of 1663, having sent requests for money to his wife, Anne, back in London, which she supplied by taking out loans that would remain unrepaid years later.

Revels as a sweetener (*BD*, vol. 7, p. 125), a post he retained until his death in 1704, having retired from the theatre in 1678. He was, presumably, also promised more significant acting roles by Davenant.

These two factors – Killigrew's new theatre and dissatisfaction within the Duke's Company's ranks – loomed large in Davenant's mind as he proceeded to develop repertory for LIF in the ensuing months. His first production following Harris's return to the company after the ruckus was Shakespeare and Fletcher's *Henry VIII*, sometime around 22 December 1663 (*LS*, p. 73). The play provided ample opportunities for scenic and musical display but given the febrile off-stage atmosphere at LIF Davenant also needed to be sensitive as to how he set about casting his actors in it. Betterton, unsurprisingly, took the role of the King, if only on account of his stocky physique, never mind his position as the leading actor. Harris, on the other hand, was offered the chance to play Cardinal Wolsey (Figure 1), which is, on paper at least, a more demanding and thus rewarding part than he had previously undertaken at LIF, complete with soliloquies and a tragic downfall (Roberts 2010, p. 93). Davenant's casting was distinctly double-edged, however: central to the plot is Wolsey's fall from grace; he is presented throughout the play as extremely 'cunning' (Shakespeare 2005, 1.1.168), self-serving, and greedy; and the central scene (Act 3, scene 2) shows the Cardinal accused of scheming with the Pope and thus of disloyalty to his monarch. As Wolsey bids farewell to his privileged position at court, for instance, he is forced to beg for Henry's forgiveness in the most humiliating and obsequious terms:

> My sovereign, I confess your royal graces
> Showered on me daily have been more than could
> My studied purposes requite, which went
> Beyond all man's endeavours. My endeavours
> Have ever come too short of my desires,
> Yet filed with my abilities. Mine own ends
> Have been mine so that evermore they pointed
> To th' good of your most sacred person and
> The profit of the state. For your great graces,
> Heaped upon me, poor undeserver, I
> Can nothing render but allegiant thanks,

Shakespeare and the Restoration Repertory 39

Figure 1 Henry Harris as Cardinale Wolsey in *Henry VIII*. Print by Henry Dawe after the painting by John Greenhill, published by W.J. White, 1820.

> My prayers to heaven for you, my loyalty,
> Which ever has and ever shall be growing,
> Till death, that winter, kill it.
>
> (Shakespeare 2005, 3.2.167–80)

David Roberts (2010, pp. 92–95) finds parallels between the Cardinal's situation here and Harris's own in his recent reconciliation (or capitulation) with his manager and his company. While he enjoyed playing a more substantial role, Harris was nevertheless required to eat a large slice of humble pie. Just as Wolsey comes to acknowledge that he owes everything he has to the benevolence of the King, so 'Harris emerged from his dispute with Davenant' (Roberts 2010, pp. 94) – he too had finally to submit to the manager's authority, despite his pride, and offer 'allegiant thanks'. As King Henry/Betterton looked on, Harris's subordinate position within the company was made manifest through blocking and stage layout. This on-stage power struggle between the two actors would continue to be exploited through Davenant's future casting decisions to powerful effect. In Orrery's *Henry the Fifth* (September 1664), for instance, Harris finally took on a kingly role himself, playing against Betterton as Owen Tudor. In the same playwright's *Mustapha* (1665), a sequel to Davenant's *The Siege of Rhodes*, Betterton reprised the part of Solyman the Magnificent, with Harris playing the title role, Solyman's son. Roberts (2010, pp. 95–97) traces how the rivalry led to these and other productive performances.

Henry VIII was thus an important production for the Duke's Company, given its role in re-establishing internal hierarchies and re-affirming, if only tentatively, interpersonal bonds between its actors and management after the disruption caused by Harris's strike. But the play also served as 'a direct challenge to Killigrew and his company' (Miyoshi 2012, p. 16). Downes (1987, pp. 55–56) records that the production was carefully rehearsed and elaborately decorated in order to showcase LIF to best advantage:

Figure 1 (Cont.)

ART File H314 no.1. Folger Shakespeare Library. Reproduced courtesy of the Folger Shakespeare Library, Washington, DC, under a Creative Commons Attribution-ShareAlike 4.0 International License.

> This Play, by Order of *Sir William Davenant*, was all new Cloath'd in proper Habits: The King's was new, all the Lords, the Cardinals, the Bishops, the Doctors, Proctors, Lawyers, Tip-staves, new Scenes: The part of the King was so right and justly done by Mr *Betterton*, he being Instructed in it by Sir *William*, who had it from Old Mr. *Lowen*, that had his Instructions from Mr. *Shakespear* himself, that I dare and will aver, none can, or will come near him in this Age, in the performance of that part: Mr. *Harris*'s performance of Cardinal *Wolsey*, was little Inferior to that, he doing it with such just State, Port, and Mein, that I dare affirm, none hitherto has Equall'd him [...] Every part by the great Care of Sir *William*, being exactly perform'd; it being all new Cloath'd and new Scenes; it continu'd Acting 15 Days together with general Applause.

As Richard Schoch (2016, p. 156) has observed, the striking thing about Downes's account is 'the distinction between what was *new* in the performance and what was *old*'. On the one hand, Downes clearly saw Davenant as somehow preserving or curating an acting style that had its roots back in the authentically Shakespearean: John Lowin (1576–1653) had been a prominent member of the pre-war King's Men, and so Davenant is understood to have guided Betterton in his part by drawing on his own memories of Lowin's original performances, which were overseen by Shakespeare himself (unlike Downes's anecdote [1987, pp. 51–52] about Shakespeare instructing John Taylor in *Hamlet*, this timeline is possible). In other words, Davenant self-consciously laid claim to the 'antebellum traditions of performance' (Miyoshi 2012, p. 16) that had come to be so closely associated with Killigrew's company, made up, as it was, of old King's Men members (and therefore one-time colleagues of Lowin). On the other hand, Downes celebrates Davenant for investing heavily in the novel elements of the Restoration stage. His account highlights the impressive visuals of the production that enhanced the play's many processions, pageants, and majestic tableaux to the delight of spectators. It is easy to imagine, for instance, how he could utilize the specially commissioned scenery and costumes with music and lighting effects to generate the complex stage picture of the trial scene (Act 2, scene 4):

> *Trumpets, Sennet, and Cornets.*
> *Enter two Vergers with short silver wands; next them two Scribes in the habit of Doctors; after them the Bishop of Canterbury alone; after him, the Bishops of Lincoln, Ely, Rochester, and S. Asaph: Next them, with some small distance, followes a Gentleman bearing the Purse, with the great Seale, and a Cardinals Hat: Then two Priests bearing each a Silver Crosse: Then a Gentleman Usher, bare-headed, accompanyed with a Sergeant at Armes, bearing a Silver Mace: Then two Gentlemen bearing two great Silver Pillers: After them, side by side, the two Cardinals, two Noblemen, with the Sword and Mace. The King takes place under the Cloth of State. The two Cardinalls sit under him as Judges. The Queene takes place some distance from the King. The Bishops place themselves on each side the Court in manner of a Consistory: Below them the Scribes. The Lords sit next the Bishops. The rest of the Attendants stand in convenient order about the Stage.*

(Shakespeare 1623, sig. V2 r)

The emphasis here on costume, music, and stage movement would inform many future productions at LIF.

Henry VIII thus contributed to the establishment of a dramaturgical house style that would come to characterize Davenant's productions going forward: these would be beautifully designed, with an emphasis on sartorial and scenic verisimilitude, often with a historical setting, all meticulously rehearsed and performed by consummate professionals.[11] Moreover, the

---

[11] Not everyone was convinced. Pepys thought it was 'so simple a thing, made up of a great many patches, that, besides the shows and processions in it, there is nothing in the world good or well done' (1995, vol. 5, p. 2; 1 January 1664). Katherine Philips apparently echoed wider opinion in a letter dated 22 January 1664 to her friend, Lady Temple, when she wrote that 'Harry ye 8th &

production announced that Shakespeare would be a central tenet of Davenant's repertory in a way that his rivals would never countenance; given what we know about the other plays staged at LIF during this season, *Henry VIII* had by far the longest run and was the most expensive play to produce.[12] The Duke's Company's players, then, despite their youth and relative inexperience, were, as Downes insists, capable of honouring their theatrical heritage (acting tradition) while simultaneously embracing the latest innovations (theatrical spectacle).

This house style is also in evidence at the other end of the season, which Davenant closed with another premiere, this time of a play by Orrery, who was quickly becoming a favourite writer of both companies (Orrery 1937, pp. 22–50; Watkins, forthcoming). *Henry the Fifth* bears little relation to Shakespeare's *Henry V*, which was never performed in the Restoration, and is cast more in the mould of the love-and-honour plots of earlier Duke's Company heroic plays such as *The Siege of Rhodes*, *Law Against Lovers*, and

some later ones [i.e. recent Davenant productions]' were 'little better than Puppett-plays' (cited but misdated [24 Jan] in *LS*, p. 74; cf. Milhous and Hume 1991, vol. 1, #267). Philips never saw the production for herself, however, being in Wales at the time, and she was predisposed to paint Davenant's endeavours in the blackest terms because of a perceived slight against her own work: sometime soon after this letter, the Duke's Company staged *Pompey the Great*, a translation of Corneille's *Pompée* (1642) by Edmund Waller, Charles Sackville, Sir Charles Sedley, and others at court, instead of her own translation from the previous year (which Davenant had in the meantime burlesqued in Act 5 of *Playhouse to be Let*).

[12] The performance calendar is frustratingly incomplete for 1663–4, but we can combine the dates we do have with publications of new plays to ascertain which works received a premiere in this season. Along with *Henry VIII*, the other plays introduced to the repertory were: Henry Cary's *The Marriage Night* (1 recorded performance); Robert Stapylton's *The Step-Mother* (2 – 1 at LIF and 1 at court); Edmund Waller et al's *Pompey the Great* (2 – at court); William Shakespeare's *King Lear* (1); Richard Flecknoe's *Love's Kingdom* (1); George Etherege's *The Comical Revenge* (1 – but Downes [1987, p. 57] suggests it made £1000, implying around 15 performances); *Heraclius* (1 – not printed); *The German Princess* (1 – not printed); *Worse and Worse* (1 – not printed); Orrery's *Henry the Fifth* (10 [Downes 1987, p. 61]).

Adventure of Five Hours. In rhymed couplets, the play charts the rivalry of King Henry and Owen Tudor for the love of Princess Katherine, daughter of the French Queen, echoing Charles II's recent courtship of Catherine of Braganza. Henry is presented as a 'romanticized portrait of Charles II – handsome and adventuresome', according to Nancy Klein Maguire (1992, p. 175). The play clearly formed part of Davenant's larger project in this season for well-turned-out historical romances. *Henry the Fifth*, like *Henry VIII*, placed great emphasis on the production's verisimilitude and stage picture. Downes (1987, p. 61) reported that 'This Play was Spendidly Cloath'd: The King, in the Duke of *York*'s Coronation Suit: *Owen Tudor*, in King *Charles*'s: Duke of *Burgundy*, in the Lord of *Oxford*'s, and the rest all New'. The company had already made use of the coronation robes worn by the royals at Westminster Abbey on St George's Day 1661 in performances of *Love and Honour* in October that year (*LS*, p. 41), and they obviously felt that it would be appropriate to reuse them again now.[13]

Henry the Fifth was thus part of LIF's new house style, following *Henry VIII*. Harris was now given the title role; as a proxy for the louche and rakish Charles II, this suited his experience with romantic leads. Betterton instead played the rather more grounded Owen Tudor, who better suited the line in world-weary misanthropes he had been cultivating for some time with Hamlet, Mercutio, and Bosola. Mary Betterton played Queen Katherine, once again Harris's onstage lover, albeit here courted too by Thomas Betterton's Tudor. Indeed, having replaced Davenport in *The Bondman* from April 1662, Mary Betterton began to alternate between playing Thomas's lover and Harris's; she had married Thomas sometime around October 1662 (Roberts 2010, pp. 91–92). Such casting might suggest that Harris had finally overtaken Betterton in terms of precedent for leading roles. As Harris's Wolsey had been humbled in *Henry VIII*, so was

---

[13] While Davenant appears to have taken pains to ensure historically accurate or, at least, stylistically appropriate costumes for both *Henry VIII* and *Henry the Fifth*, this was not necessarily a foundational artistic policy. In her letter to Lady Temple, Philips wrote of a court performance of the collaboratively written *Pompey*: 'I heare they acted in English habits, & y^t so aprope y^t Caesar was sent in with his feather & Muff, till he was hiss'd off ye Stage' (quoted in *LS*, p. 74).

Betterton's Tudor put in his place by the end of *Henry the Fifth*: 'In Vertue, Sir [King Henry], so much you me out-shine | That you all other Motives may decline,' he says (Orrery 1937, 5.1.224–5). Nevertheless, Harris was still required to play nice with his 'best Friend' (1.1.43) Betterton. Indeed, if the latter was anxious about his displacement from kingly parts, his costuming might have alleviated his very worst fears: Downes tells us that Harris, as the king, sported the robes of his theatre's patron, the Duke of York, possibly in a show of obedience and gratitude following James's role in his return to LIF the previous summer, while Betterton, despite playing a lower-ranking part, was dressed in the finest robes of all – those of Charles II himself. As a new and popular play by a new and popular playwright, *Henry the Fifth*, like the equally successful *Henry VIII*, was used to play out the power dynamics between the company's two leading men.

Davenant's earlier experience with the Shakespeare-Fletcher *Henry VIII* may have encouraged him to adapt another of their collaborations (Roberts 2010, p. 95): he opened his next season, 1664–5, with his adaptation of *The Two Noble Kinsmen*, *The Rivals*, on 10 September (*LS*, p. 83).[14] This production would have been in rehearsals during the previous August, when *Henry the Fifth* was playing, and it shares a number of similar ideas to the latter play, but these have been obscured by confusion about its original casting. *The Rivals* was first printed in quarto in 1668, some four years after its premiere. The cast-list included in that edition lists Betterton and Harris as Philander (Palamon) and Theocles (Arcite) respectively but goes on to name Anne Shadwell, née Gibbs, as Heraclia (Emilia). But this arrangement must have been for a later revival, probably after the reopening of the theatres following the plague and Great Fire of 1665–6; we know that the play was performed, for example, on 19 November 1667, with Charles II in attendance (*LS*, p. 124). Pepys, however, implies that Mary Betterton played Heraclia in the initial run in 1664; he praised 'the good actings of Baterton and his wife and Harris' when he saw the play on

---

[14] We do not know if Davenant – or anyone in the Restoration period – was aware that Fletcher had a hand in *Henry VIII*; *The Two Noble Kinsmen*, in contrast, was printed in quarto in 1634 with both playwrights' names announced on the title page.

2 December that year (1995, vol. 5, p. 335). This trio makes particular sense in the wake of *Henry the Fifth* the month before, where they were similarly presented as a ménage à trois. Indeed, the adaptation reworks the Shakespeare-Fletcher original to bring it more closely in line with the love-and-honour spectacles associated with LIF heroic dramas and tragicomedies at this time. Where the original's Arcite dies in Act 5, in *The Rivals* both men are saved and reconciled by the play's end. In order to diffuse tensions between them, Philander eventually (and a little too effortlessly) 'transplants' (Davenant 1668, p. 56) his love and desire from Heraclia to Celania, the Provost's Daughter (Jailor's Daughter in the original), who has gone mad for love of him.[15] This compromise leaves Harris's Theocles free finally to marry Heraclia, and thus end the 'quarrel' between the two men: 'I loose a Rival and Preserve a Freind [*sic*]' (p. 56), Philander concludes. All this echoes strikingly the situation in Orrery's earlier play where Tudor (Betterton), caught between his love for Katherine (Mary Betterton) and his duty to his friend and sovereign, Henry V (Harris), falls on his sword, despite the King's promise to advocate on his behalf to Katherine, in order to enable the English monarch to marry her and thus make a politically advantageous match: 'You speak for me, but I resign for you' (5.4.330), he tells the King.

The Rivals was thus adjusted in order to replay the interpersonal relationships and casting logics established by the earlier plays: like *The Siege of Rhodes* and *Henry the Fifth*, here Betterton and Harris compete for Mary Betterton's affections, with the latter securing her hand by the end of the play

---

[15] Celania was originally played by Winifred Gosnell (*fl.*1662–97), who joined the Duke's Company in March 1663 as a bit-part actress; she took a walk-on role in *Hamlet* (*BD*, vol. 6, p. 278), for example, and was named as the singer of 'Ah, Love is a delicate ting', which she sang with a French accent, in *Playhouse to be Let* in August 1663 (Davenant 1673, p. 86; second pagination). She had worked in the Pepys household as a maid prior to her stage career, and he noted that she 'hath a good voice and sings very well, besides other good qualities' such as dancing (Pepys 1995, vol. 3, p. 256). Montague Summers (1922, pp. xxxix–xl), usually such an astute interpreter of Restoration performance records, inexplicably suggests that Mary Betterton originally played Celania in 1664.

while the former nobly steps aside. We can see that *The Rivals* also conforms to Davenant's preferred house style in its dramaturgy. Like *Henry VIII* and, more especially, *Law Against Lovers*, *The Rivals* boasts many opportunities for the kinds of stage pageantry and musical entertainment that was becoming synonymous in the minds of audiences with LIF productions. Downes (1987, p. 55) noted that the play had 'a very Fine Interlude in it, of Vocal and Instrumental Musick, mixt with very Diverting Dances'. This likely refers to Act 3, where the script calls for one actor-dancer, probably Joseph Price (*fl.* 1661–97?), to perform a country jig, before three pairs of countrymen and women perform a Morris dance in front of Arcon, the Prince of Arcadia, and his entourage (pp. 33–34).[16] Alternatively, Downes might have in mind the highpoint of musical spectacle in Act 4: a deer hunt in a wood, in which 'Musick expresses the Chase by Voices and Instruments like hollaing and winding of Horns' (Davenant 1668, p. 38); it concludes with '*our Dance, wherein we have no small-hope, Because it does both Amble, Trot and Gallop*' (p. 39). The reputed dancing master, Luke Channel (*fl.* 1653–91), was formally sworn into the Duke's Company on 23 November 1664, but was very likely working at LIF quite some time before this, and it might be the case that *The Rivals* was one of the first productions he worked on (Downes 1987, p. 71n209; Milhous and Hume 1991, #155). Channel had already composed a jig for Sir George Etherege's *The Comical Revenge* the previous spring (*LS*, p. 76) at LIF – the tune 'Love in a Tub, *or* Luke Cheynell's Jigg' appeared in the musical miscellany *Apollo's Banquet* in 1670 – so he would have been perfectly capable of devising this kind of terpsichorean display. (Channel would go on to choreograph the witches' dances for *Macbeth* in November 1664, discussed later.)

[16] According to Downes (1987, p. 55), Price spoke 'a short Comical Prologue' introducing the dances in Acts 3 and 4, which 'gain'd him an Universal Applause of the Town'. These interludes are indeed introduced by a 'Countrey-Poet' who functions as '*Master of the Revels*' in Q1668 (p. 35), and Price could easily have performed this role and danced the jig mentioned earlier, despite not being named in the 1668 cast-list. The Country Poet's speeches are quite perfunctory, however, so perhaps Price recited an unrecorded or ad-libbed speech that gained the audience's applause; as a rustic poet, this would not have been inappropriate for the character.

While Davenant was building up his actors' dance skills, he was also showcasing their strengths as singers. In Act 3, Theocles is required to sing 'Under the Willow Shades they were', while Celania is called to sing seven songs over the course of the play; indeed, Celania is 'distracted' (i.e. mad) throughout much of the action, often resembling Ophelia, and this is given as the motivation for her musical outbursts. In Restoration theatre, singing tended to be reserved for the mad, the melancholic, or the magical (Plank 1990; Eubanks Winkler 2006). Her Act 5 showpiece, 'My lodging it is on the Cold ground', was sung by Winifred Gosnell at the premiere, when Pepys reported that, despite usually singing and dancing so finely, here she 'fell out of Key, so that the Musique could not play to her afterward'. In response, her duet partner, Harris, tried to salvage the situation by following her 'out of the tune to agree with her', but evidently even his musicality could not retrieve the performance ('Pepys 1995, vol. 5, p. 267; 10 September 1664). While both Celania and Theocles are required to sing individually, there is no cue for a duet for them anywhere in the 1668 text; indeed, as Mary Edmond (1987, p. 189) notes, they share no dialogue in the play at all. Perhaps what Pepys heard on that opening night was cut from subsequent performances, given the onstage debacle at the premiere, and thus was left out of the printed edition. Regardless, soon after this performance, Gosnell was dismissed from LIF, to be replaced in the role by a much more assured singer, Moll Davis; it was Davis who was listed in the 1668 cast-list. In this way, the part of Celania might be seen as a natural progression from Viola in *Law Against Lovers*, which was sung two seasons before by the young Davis. Downes (1987, p. 55) recorded that when the King heard her sing 'My lodging it is on the Cold ground' in a 1667 revival of the play, Davis 'perform'd that so Charmingly, that not long after, it Rais'd her from her Bed on the Cold Ground, to a Bed Royal'. Indeed, she became his mistress for a brief period that winter (*BD*, vol. 4, pp. 222–226).

4 Supernatural Rivals

As Tiffany Stern (2000, p. 140) observes, in the Restoration period 'new plays were slowly added to the repertoire between September and November, so that more careful (and more frequent) rehearsal took place at the beginning of the season'. With *The Rivals* opening the LIF 1664–5 season in September, Davenant offered a well-prepared addition in the by-now familiar house style of the Duke's Company: a love-and-honour plot revolving around Thomas Betterton, Mary Betterton, and Henry Harris; scenic verisimilitude, in the form of the forest and prison scenes; and competently executed performances, including dance numbers and songs (albeit with an unfortunate vocal performance by Gosnell on opening night). The company's next new production was indeed introduced into the repertory in November and was yet another Shakespeare adaptation that required even more extensive rehearsals: *Macbeth* (*LS*, p. 85). *Macbeth* may have been deliberately scheduled to coincide with Gunpowder Plot Day. Pepys (1995, vol. 5, p. 314) records first seeing it on 5 November: 'to the Duke's house to a play, *Macbeth*; a pretty good play, but admirably acted. Thence home, the coach being forced to go round by London-wall home because of the Bonfires – the day being mightily observed in the City.'

Davenant's alterations to this play worked, once again, to bring it in line with his growing repertory of Fletcherian tragicomedies and heroic dramas. Like the two *Rhodes* plays, as printed in 1663, for example, *Macbeth* centres on two opposing married couples – the Macduffs now substantially developed and serving as foils for the Macbeths – while the two male characters meditate on how best to reconcile uxorious love with public duty and personal honour. It presented audiences with a corrupt, but compelling, usurper-regicide who is ultimately thwarted by the restoration of the rightful heir, Malcolm, echoing the themes of many plays – new *and* old stock – that were an increasingly large proportion of both houses' offerings at this point (Maguire 1992, pp. 64–78). Moreover, as in *Henry VIII* and *Henry the Fifth*, Davenant selected a play founded on (mytho-)historical materials.[17] Finally, Davenant's adaptation invested heavily in the dramaturgical and aesthetic elements of the wider LIF repertory: in its newly composed scenes, Davenant's *Macbeth* eschewed Shakespearean blank verse in favour of the

[17] The play's publisher, Peter Chetwin, emphasized the story's historical origins by including the relevant passage on Macbeth from Peter Heylin's *Cosmographie in Four Books* as 'The Argument' in Q1674. Heylin's work was first published in 1652 but was reprinted in 1674, with Chetwin's involvement (Spencer 1965, p. 403).

rhymed heroic couplet (as had *The Siege of Rhodes*, *Law Against Lovers*, and *Henry the Fifth* before it), and it deployed the full range of scenic and musical technologies available at the theatre to create its spectacular effects in the form of dance pageants and processions, such the '*shaddow of eight Kings*' (Davenant 1674, p. 48) that concludes Act 4, scene 1 (Figure 2).

While this all suggests that *Macbeth* shared much with the heroic plays that preceded it, it nevertheless presented a marked departure from LIF house style in one very crucial particular: its spectacular interludes concerned supernatural characters – the witches – who demonstrate their magical qualities through song and dance in Act 2, scene 5, Act 3, scene 8, and Act 4, scene 1. Notoriously, the first scene closes with the witches exiting on wires, '*flying*' (Davenant 1674, 1.1.10SD), and while this may reflect a later production at the Dorset Garden theatre in 1673 – as we have seen, it is likely that LIF did not have a rope-pulley system, while the later theatre certainly did – Christopher Spencer (1969) nevertheless argues that what was produced at LIF in November 1664 was essentially Davenant's adaptation as it survives in both its printed and manuscript versions.[18] He reached this conclusion by showing that Act 1 of *The Rivals* contains a number of verbal echoes and imitations of *Macbeth*, in both its original and adapted forms, suggesting Davenant worked on both plays simultaneously (i.e. over the winter and spring of 1663–4). Regardless of how the witches entered the stage at LIF, then, they certainly proved to be a major attraction for audiences. Pepys (1995, vol. 8, p. 7) wrote that *Macbeth* was 'a most excellent play in all respects, but especially in divertisement' when he saw it yet again on 7 January 1667.

Remarkably, no play prior to *Macbeth* at LIF included supernatural/magical characters that demanded musical or scenic spectacle on the scale of

---

[18] As well as Q1674, there is also the manuscript version of the play held at the University of Yale, which Spencer (1961, pp. 38–54) dates to 1663 or 1664, despite its title page declaring a date of '1674'. This version contains all the song and music cues found in Q1674, as well as the opening '*flying*' direction and signals for machine effects at 3.8.21SD and 4.1.29D, but its relationship to a datable production is impossible to verify.

Figure 2 Frontispiece to *Macbeth* from Nicholas Rowe's *Works* (1709).
Source Call Number: ART File S528m1 no.53. Folger Shakespeare

this production.[19] Indeed, such supernaturalism seems to have gone against Davenant's aesthetic principles as both playwright and theatre manager up to this point. As long ago as 1650, he had argued in the *Preface* to *Gondibert* against the poet or playwright who depicted 'conversations with Gods and Ghosts' because that ultimately 'deprives us of those naturall probabilities in Story, which are instructive to humane life' (Davenant 1971, p. 4). Instead, he insisted on writing poems and plays that would civilize the people through rational and verisimilar narratives, whose morals they could easily apply to their own circumstances. Dramatists 'prevail most on our manners', he wrote, 'when they lay the Scene at home in their owne Country' and 'avoid those remote regions of Heaven and Hell' (Davenant 1971, p. 5). As a consequence of this focus on the verisimilar, 'the People' are made 'civill by an easy communication with reason' and thus 'become more discreet than to have their eyes persuaded by the descending of Gods in gay Clowds, and more manly than to be frighted with the rising of Ghosts in Smoake' (Davenant 1971, p. 5).

Such statements no doubt resulted from the particular context in which Davenant was writing in the 1650s; after all, the *Preface* was addressed to the rationalist philosopher Thomas Hobbes, who had himself dismissed superstitious attachment to the occult in chapter 45 of *Leviathan*, written in the same year and read in draft by the poet. Nevertheless, Davenant does appear

Figure 2 (Cont.)

Library. Reproduced courtesy of the Folger Shakespeare Library, Washington, DC, under a Creative Commons Attribution-ShareAlike 4.0 International License.

[19] Spencer (1965, p. 406) notes that the scene in which the divine omens are heard from Mars and Venus in *The Two Noble Kinsmen* (Act 5, scene 1) is conspicuously cut from *The Rivals*. I discount the appearance of ghosts of dead humans, like Old Hamlet and Banquo, from my argument here as they do not provoke the same kinds of theatrical spectacle as other supernatural figures, such as gods, witches, and magicians.

to have carried his antipathy towards the supernatural into the Restoration period too (Watkins 2023b, pp. 55–56; Hubbard 2024, pp. 54–56). *Hamlet* certainly contains a ghost, but he does not rise from below the stage in smoke, nor does he descend from the ceiling 'in gay Clowds' at LIF; instead, the text states that the ghost simply enters and exits the stage like other characters – although he 'cries under the Stage' in Act 1, scene 5 (p. 21).

As we have already seen, then, Davenant's theatre did not possess these kinds of machine technologies, and so he avoided plays that called for such fantastical manoeuvres. The closest an LIF production prior to November 1664 came to supernaturalism was Robert Stapylton's *The Step-Mother*. Performed a year before *Macbeth*, sometime in the autumn of 1663 (*LS*, p. 71), Stapylton's tragicomedy revolves around Pontia (played by Mrs. Williams),[20] newly married to the weak-willed Prince of Verulam. She attempts to usurp her husband and remove his children from the succession, instead securing the crown for herself and her son. In order to learn whether her plans will succeed, she makes a visit to a cave where she receives an ambiguous prophecy from a bard, a conjuror, and a witch (Stapylton 1664, pp. 22–23). Pontia comes away from this encounter believing these figures to be real magical beings, insisting that the bard, for example, 'be somewhat more then humane, | He speaks the Language of another World, | So well; that his expressions are all Picture' (p. 24). However, the audience already knows that this is not the case: the scene is in fact a deception, perpetrated by the loyal servants of the Prince's faction, Tetrick (played by Cave Underhill) and Fromund (Joseph Price), to incriminate the Princess. Indeed, Pontia's own general, Crispus, indicates that he sees through the illusion when he advises her that 'our *Bards* | (Like all the tribe of Fortune-tellers) [are] Juglers' (p. 24). She dismisses his concerns and proceeds with her design until all is resolved (happily) at the play's conclusion. Later, in one of a number of elaborate masques performed throughout the play, Pontia enters dressed as the goddess Diana to sing and dance alongside her

---

[20] The only other role associated with Mrs. Williams (*fl.* 1663–68) is Leandra in *The Slighted Maid*, also by Stapylton and performed in February 1663 (*BD*, vol. 16, p. 134).

daughter, Caesarina (Mary Betterton) as Flora, and her favourite, Brianella (Jane Long) as Progne (p. 59).

The selection of Stapylton's play shows how reluctant Davenant was to present audiences with actual demonstrations of supernaturalism on the LIF stage; on the rare occasion he did showcase divine or magical characters, they were revealed to be either frauds and tricksters, comically entrapping the villain of the piece, or as morally reformed royals celebrating their reintegration into civilized court life. (In this way, Stapylton's masques echo the kinds of entertainments danced at the Stuart court prior to 1642, where they were performed by courtiers dressed as mythical and classical figures; Davenant, who commissioned Stapylton, had of course served as the chief masque librettist at the Caroline court.) This was no doubt partly a result of the theatrical limitations of LIF itself (no machines to make such characters credible), and partly because Davenant was committed to a form of theatre that presented audiences with narratives of *human* actions and passions – love, honour, duty, betrayal, credulousness – from which they might derive some (self-)knowledge. The question thus remains: why, in the autumn of 1664, did Davenant abandon his artistic policy against stage supernaturalism and produce a play in which genuine witches danced and sang?

The answer, I want to suggest, lies in what Killigrew had been doing with his company over the first few years of his operation. If Davenant's early repertory consisted of love-and-honour tragicomedies and verisimilar heroic dramas at the expense of supernatural plays, this was definitely not the case with his rivals at the King's Company. Plays containing a significant magical component had been a frequent presence there since its earliest days, despite the lack of any scenic capacity at Vere Street: during the 1662 season alone, for example, Killigrew's company staged *A Midsummer Night's Dream* (*LS*, p. 55), *The Merry Devil of Edmonton* (*LS*, p. 31), and *Bussy D'Ambois* (*LS*, p. 45), complete with its diabolic spirits, Behemoth and Cartophylax.[21] They followed this up after the move to Bridges Street with a production of *The Faithful Shepherdess*, which

[21] Perhaps Killigrew's penchant for devilish characters stemmed from his own experiences of the theatre as a child, as recounted by Pepys: 'He would go to the Red-bull, and when the man cried to the boys, "Who will go and be a divell, and

boasts a satyr, a river god, and a magical fountain (*LS*, p. 66). Indeed, it was the move to Bridges Street that enabled Killigrew to go even further in this direction in order to showcase just what the new theatre could do in terms of stage spectacle. As a result, in 1663 he commissioned a new play from a hot young talent, John Dryden, and his brother-in-law, Sir Robert Howard.[22] They came up with *The Indian Queen*, which was eventually performed on 24 January 1664, going up directly against Davenant's production of *Henry VIII*; it ran for ten consecutive nights (*LS*, pp. 74–75). Killigrew's timing seems to have worked in his favour. On 27 January 1664, Pepys (1995, vol. 5, pp. 28–29) found 'the street full of coaches at the new play, *The Indian Queene*; which for show, they say, exceeds *Henry the 8th*'.

The Indian Queen was lavishly decorated and presented its audiences with stunning scenic effects, music, and costumes (Figure 3). Like *Henry VIII*, the production invested heavily in spectacle. A record for a warrant to the Master of the Great Wardrobe asked for £40 of silk 'to cloath the Musick for the play called the Indian Queene to be acted before their Majesties Jan. 25th 1663 [/4]'. A particular highlight noted by contemporary commentators was the discovery of the Temple of the Sun in Act 5: '*The Scene opens, and discovers the Temple of the Sun all of Gold, and four Priests in habits of white and red Feathers attending by a bloody Altar, as ready for sacrifice*' (5.1.0SD). In her romance, *Oroonoko* (1688), Aphra Behn (1997, p. 9) intimates that she furnished the King's Company with some 'unimitable' feathers that she had picked up on her travels to South America for 'the Dress of the *Indian Queen*'. This was probably for a revival of the play in 1668, but it nevertheless indicates the level of colourful spectacle demanded by the production.

When John Evelyn saw the production in February, he described it as 'a Tragedie well written, but so beautified with rich Scenes as the like had never ben seene here as happly (except rarely any where else) on

he shall see the play for nothing?" – then would he go and be a devil upon the stage, and so got to see [the] play' (1995, vol. 3, pp. 243–244; 30 October 1662).

[22] Howard's contribution to *The Indian Queen* was limited, despite the play first appearing in his *Four New Works* in 1665. Its modern editors, rightly in my view, identify Dryden as its dominant, even exclusive, author (Dryden 1956–2002, vol. 8, p. 283).

Figure 3 Anne Bracegirdle as the Indian Queen. Print by William Vincent, published by J. Smith, c.1689–99. ART 232–569.1. Folger Shakespeare Library. Reproduced courtesy of the Folger Shakespeare Library, Washington, DC, under a Creative Commons Attribution-ShareAlike 4.0 International License.

a mercenarie Theater' (quoted in *LS*, p. 75). James A. Winn (1987, p. 145) notes that the play 'catered to the public taste for spectacle, which the new theatre was finally able to satisfy'.

Dryden and Howard's play was remarkable for the sophistication with which it handled the stock themes of earlier tragicomedies and heroic plays. Set in Peru, *The Indian Queen* follows the actions of the usurping monarch of the title, Zempoalla, who takes control of Peru after her Mexican forces overthrow its legitimate monarch, the Inca, and his daughter, Orazia. Over the course of the play, Zempoalla is caught between her desire to kill her rivals in a ritual sacrifice and her love for the Peruvian general, Montezuma, who turned coat after the conquest but who still harbours ambitions to marry Orazia. As the various love triangles and political conflicts resolve themselves, the play restores the status quo by having Zempoalla commit suicide alongside her son, leaving the stage clear for the return of the rightful ruler, the Incan king. In the play's closing moments Montezuma finally learns from a messenger that he is, in fact, no mere soldier but rather the son and heir of the recently murdered Mexican king, Zempoalla's predecessor. We are told that the old king

> bred you [Montezuma] in a Cave,
> But kept the mighty secret from your ear
> Lest heat of blood so some strange course shou'd steer
> Your youth—'[23]

(Dryden 1956–2002, vol. 8, 5.1.237–40)

All ends happily, in true Fletcherian mode, with the two proper monarchs finally restored to their thrones, joined together in political amity through the impending marriage of Orazia and Montezuma. It was, however, its groundbreaking use of supernatural spectacle that made *The Indian Queen* a major milestone in the development of the heroic play as a theatrical genre.

The coup de théâtre came in the central scene, Act 3, scene 2, when Zempoalla, concerned to learn more about her future prospects with

---

[23] This scenario no doubt informed Dryden's portrayal of Hippolito, who is similarly kept isolated in a cave until he is ready to take on his role as duke of Mantua, in *The Tempest, or the Enchanted Island* (1667).

Montezuma, travels to the 'dismal Cell' (3.2.2) of the prophet Ismeron. Here, she asks him to summon up the God of Sleep and thereby reveal '*what strange Fate | Must on her dismal Vision wait*' (3.2.70–71). Ismeron then proceeds to recite an elaborate incantation:

> *By the croaking of the Toad,*
> *In their Caves that make aboad,*
> *Earthy* Dun *that pants for breath,*
> *With her well'd sides full of death;*
> *By the Crested Adders Pride*
> *That along the Clifts do glide;*
> *By thy visage fierce and black;*
> *By the Deaths-head on thy back;*
> *By the twisted Serpents place'd*
> *For a Girdle round thy Waste;*
> *By the Hearts of Gold that deck*
> *Thy Brest, thy Shoulders, and thy Neck:*
> *From thy sleepy Mansion rise,*
> *And open thy unwilling Eyes,*
> *While bubling Springs their Musick keep,*
> *That use to lull thee in thy sleep.*

(3.2.79–94)

This leads to the appearance of the god, who rises from a trapdoor underneath the stage and advises Zempoalla to 'Seek not to know what must not be reveal'd' (3.2.95); 'All must', he insists, 'submit to their appointed doom' (3.2.103) without divine knowledge. He then descends, before some 'Ariel-Spirits' (3.2.118SD) sing a finale, suspended from wires overhead. Realizing that these 'Charms of Music' (3.2.117) will not furnish her with the knowledge (or reassurance) she craves, Zempoalla dismisses them as 'Trifles' (3.2.131) and threatens to burn 'all their Temples into ashes' (3.2.142), before storming off.

We can see that this scene from Dryden and Howard's play echoes Pontia's visit to the Bard's cave in Stapylton's *The Step-Mother*, which was on stage as they were writing it. But there are crucial differences: in *The Indian Queen*, the

God of Sleep and Ariel-Spirits are, within the logic of the play-world, genuinely supernatural, and Zempoalla dismisses what they eventually tell her; in Stapylton's play, the conjuror and witch are fake, but Pontia believes everything they say, despite others' scepticism. We can see Killigrew's distinct treatment of the supernatural in such cases as an early example on the Restoration stage of what Andrew R. Walkling (2019, p. 21) has termed 'diegetic supernaturalism' – that is, scenes in which the real-world audience in the theatre 'observes the [onstage] character(s) witnessing what is, within the context of their world, an "actual" supernatural event'. 'Diegetic supernaturalism' was a frequently recurring trope in later Restoration productions, particularly at the King's Company, enabling, as it did, plays to present spectators with music and spectacle in a logically coherent way; rather than having mortal men and women breaking out into song and dance for no reason, this kind of performance was reserved for supernatural characters and episodes and was witnessed by onstage spectators, who typically asserted the irrational and fictive nature of the illusions occurring in front of them. Walkling's generic label for these productions is 'spectacle-tragedy' (2019, pp. 82–116).

It would appear, then, that Davenant was consciously encroaching on Killigrew's success with spectacle-tragedy when he produced his adaptation of *Macbeth* in November 1664, ten months after the sensation of *The Indian Queen* at Bridges Street. While Zempoalla's visit to Isermon's cell may have been directly inspired by the analogous episode in *The Step-Mother*, both plays are clearly indebted to Act 4, scene 1, of Shakespeare's *Macbeth*, in which Macbeth returns to the witches in search of information about his future encounters with Macduff, only for Hecate and her apparitions to answer him with ambiguous riddles. As the modern editors of *The Indian Queen* remark: 'If Zempoalla's story had been represented from the beginning, the play would have been a tragedy and she would dominate it as a kind of female Macbeth' (Dryden 1956–2002, vol. 8, p. 294). Indeed, the witches' charm from Shakespeare's *Macbeth* seems to have served as a direct source for Dryden:

> Round about the cauldron go;
> In the poisoned entrails throw.
> Toad, that under cold stone

> Days and night has thirty-one,
> Sweltered venon sleeping got,
> Boil thou first i'th' charmed pot [...]
> Fillet of a fenny snake,
> In the cauldron boil and bake;
> Eye of newt and toe of frog,
> Wool of bat and tongue of dog,
> Adder's fork and blind-worm's sting,
> Lizard's leg and howlet's wing,
> For a charm of powerful trouble,
> Like a hell-broth boil and bubble.
>
> (Shakespeare 2005, 4.1.4–19)

The Scottish witches' recipe is more elaborate, but the essential ingredients are there in both incantations: both refer to toads, adders and serpents, bubbles, and sleep; both are in a distinctive trochaic tetrameter, isolated from the plays' more familiar iambic pentameter rhythms; and both Dryden's God of Sleep and Shakespeare's Hecate partially satisfy their visitors' enquiries before descending below the stage only to be forcefully called back. Finally, both Zempoalla and Macbeth are presented with a dramatic spectacle in which their respective fates are cryptically revealed. Neither is calmed or reassured by what they witness; instead, their respective levels of fear, anxiety, and paranoia substantially increase from this moment on. If the scene in Ismeron's cell could delight and enthral audiences by echoing so closely Shakespeare's text, Davenant surely intended to go one better by staging *Macbeth* itself, now in heroic form – that is, as a spectacle-tragedy (Watkins 2023b).[24]

Davenant's *Macbeth* displays many of the traits of 'diegetic supernaturalism' as Walkling sets it out. Whereas in Shakespeare's original the only character to raise even the slightest doubt about the witches' power is Banquo – in Shakespeare's text, Banquo asks 'Were such things here as

---

[24] James A. Winn (2004, p. 293) mistakes the direction of influence by arguing that Dryden and Howard were themselves responding to the popularity of the LIF adaptation of *Macbeth*, but he misdates the latter's first performance.

we do speak about, | Or have we eaten on the insane root | That takes the reason prisoner?' (Shakespeare 2005, 1.3.81–3), but subsequently he seems to accept the witches' prophetic powers like everybody else – in the Restoration version, onstage mortals spend significant stretches of time watching supernatural happenings and commenting on their veracity, often voicing sceptical positions at crucial moments. Most especially, Lady Macduff watches the witches singing and dancing on the heath in Act 2, scene 5, just after Duncan's murder and Macbeth's ascent to the throne. She and her husband rendezvous with a plan to 'shun the place of danger by our flight | from *Everness*' (Spencer, ed., 1965, 2.5.6–7). Before they can set off, however, they encounter the witches, who proceed to sing two ominous songs before concluding with an extended dance. The first song, 'Speak, Sister, speak', raises the idea that Duncan's murder will quickly precipitate yet further horrific crimes – 'Ill deeds are seldom slow nor single' (2.5.32) – before concluding in a chorus in which the witches declare that they 'rejoyce when good Kings bleed' (2.5.40). This is immediately followed by 'Let's have a dance upon the Heath', which again connects the witches with regicide: 'We gain more life by *Duncan's* death' (2.5.50).

As the first song concludes, Lady Macduff reveals that she has been watching not only the witches but also her husband's reaction to them:

> *La. Macd.* This is most strange: but why seem you affraid?
> Can you be capable of fears, who have
> So often caus'd it in your enemies?
> *Macd.* It was a hellish Song: I cannot dread
> Ought that is mortal; but this is something more.
>
> (2.5.44–9)

The military hero, usually the cause of fear in others, is here visibly reduced to fright by what he sees. Clearly, Macduff accepts what his senses tell him: that these figures are indeed supernatural, even diabolical, beings. Lady Macduff, by contrast, is calmer and more clear-eyed. She embodies Davenant's rationalist position as set out in the *Preface* to *Gondibert*. After the second song, she acknowledges their genuine magical powers but insists that those with blameless consciences need not be scared by what they portend: 'None can fear ill, but those that merit it' (2.5.70), she says. Secure in her moral righteousness, Lady Macduff dismisses the witches as 'nothing but fiction' and encourages her husband to 'hasten on our journey' (2.5.90–1). Macduff agrees to follow his wife's 'counsel', 'for to permit | Such thoughts upon our memories to dwell, | Will make our minds the Registers of Hell' (2.5.92–4).

Davenant incorporates this scene as a contrast to Macbeth's later encounter with the witches in Act 4, scene 1. In the earlier scene, the moral character, Lady Macduff, remains rational and sceptical, and therefore is not taken in by the witches' revelations; in the later scene, on the other hand, Macbeth, already corrupted by murder and ambition, is only too susceptible to their wily trickery. But Act 2, scene 5, also has wider implications beyond the internal dramaturgy of the individual play. Lady Macduff is in the end killed by Macbeth's order, as one of the 'Many more murders' that the witches insist must follow Duncan's death. Her husband, who displays a healthy respect for the threats of diabolical magic, will ultimately survive to welcome in the returning monarch, Malcolm. In this way, Lady Macduff's character is haunted, in Marvin Carlson's (2001) sense, by the figure of Zempoalla from *The Indian Queen*. Both characters initially dismiss the genuine magic they witness onstage only to suffer a fatal downfall as a result. Even as their reasons for scepticism are starkly contrasted – the usurping Zempoalla simply does not get the answers she wants from the God of Sleep (like Macbeth) and so disregards his words, while Lady Macduff places too much confidence in her own innocence – the logic of both plays condemns them for failing to heed the prophetic warnings that the supernatural characters offer up.

In this way, we can see that with *Macbeth*, Davenant was altering radically his dramaturgical praxis in order to mount a commercial challenge to Killigrew. Where Pontia in *The Step-Mother* was presented as all-too credulous in taking seriously the fraudulent performances of Tetrick and Fromund, Davenant now reverses this formula and condemns a character who *disbelieves* what she has seen. In other words, in the autumn and winter of 1664, Davenant momentarily capitulated to theatrical fashions, as instigated by Killigrew's production of *The Indian Queen*, and provided audiences with scenes of 'diegetic supernaturalism' over his standard plots of heroic –

that is, mortal – conflict. With Killigrew's company benefiting materially from their investment in the new scenic theatre at Bridges Street, Davenant was forced to adjust his house style – historical, verisimilar heroic plays – and instead presented audiences with what they evidently wanted, which included singing and dancing witches. *Macbeth* thus represents a significant shift in Davenant's approach to his repertory, as both a playwright and a theatre manager, over these difficult months in 1664, as he attempted to mount a commercially viable defence against the phenomenal successes Killigrew was enjoying with his new plays at Bridges Street.

5 Continuity and Innovation

Even as Davenant experimented with new approaches to spectacle in the form of 'diegetic supernaturalism' in 1664, he was always aware of his need to ensure that such scenes were amenable to his actors. Thus, *Macbeth* continued to offer members of the Duke's Company parts within their established heroic 'lines', even as it took them away from the heroic formulae of earlier productions. As was the case with *The Rivals*, however, Davenant's approach to adapting *Macbeth* has been occluded by faulty understanding about how the play was originally conceived in terms of casting. The only available cast-list for *Macbeth* was printed with the 1674 quarto, ten years after its premiere at LIF. This names Betterton as Macbeth, with Mary Betterton playing his onstage wife – parts for which they quickly became famous (Bartholomeusz 1969, pp. 14–27). Harris, as we might expect, given the way Davenant tended to cast him against Betterton in other heroic dramas, took the role of the noble Macduff, while William Smith played Banquo (Smith tended to play supporting/ companion figures to a play's lead character; see Table 1 and *BD*, vol. 14, pp. 168–173 for his roster of roles). Despite a misprint in the text, we know that Samuel Sandford cross-dressed to play 'Heccatte' (his name actually appears next to 'Ghost *of* Banquo', on the line above in Q1674).[25] Henry

---

[25] Summers (ed., 1922, p. xxxvi) reads this mistake literally. The Yale MS, however, correctly puts Sandford against 'Heccatt' (fol. 2r). Sandford certainly played Hecate in the 1673 Dorset Garden revival (Eubanks Winkler 2004, p. ix), thus

Norris, Philip Cademan, and Mathew Medbourne are also mentioned as playing Malcolm, Donalbain, and Lenox respectively. All of these actors were active in the Duke's Company in 1664 and so could have played these parts in the original run, reprising them later at Dorset Garden.

Other characters mentioned in the cast-list, however, are either left blank or are cast with actors that do not correspond to the 1664 company. Nathaniel Lee, for example, is identified as playing Duncan, but he only joined the Duke's Company in the 1670s (*BD*, vol. 9, p. 211), so Davenant must have had another actor in mind when he was adapting the play a decade earlier. Probably, he intended to cast Thomas Lilleston or his successor in the role, given his established line in old kings, dukes, and governor figures; he had most recently played the Prince in *The Rivals* but appears to have stopped acting at some point in the 1664–5 season, so, even if he were available to premiere the role of Duncan – and it is not possible to confirm this – it would have been inherited by his replacement shortly thereafter (*BD*, vol. 9, p. 296). No performers are identified as having played the three witches, but as these needed to be competent singers and dancers, it might be the case that the likes of Moll Davis and Winifred Gosnell took two of these parts (on the music, see Eubanks Winkler, ed., 2004 and Moore 1961).

Finally, Jane Long is named in the 1674 cast-list as Lady Macduff, arguably the moral centre of the entire play, given her aversion to Macbeth's tyrannous violence, her suspicions about her husband's true motives for interfering in Scotland's political crisis, and her outright scepticism of the witches' magical powers (Miller 2008; Reimers 2023). Long was indeed present in the Duke's Company roster in 1664, and so scholars such as Anne Greenfield (2013, p. 45) and Amanda Eubanks Winkler and Richard Schoch (2022, p. 99) have assumed that she premiered the part at LIF. However, a survey of her other roles from the 1663–5 seasons suggests that this was, in fact, highly unlikely. Since joining the company as one of Davenant's original actresses in 1661, Long had made a specialism of small speaking parts. I suspect, for example, that she played one

> establishing a tradition of male-drag performance in witches' roles. By the eighteenth century, all three witches in *Macbeth* were regularly played by men (see, for example, *The Daily Courant*, 29 December 1707).

of Ianthe's attendants in *The Siege of Rhodes* as well as Julietta, Claudio's mistress and Beatrice's companion, in *The Law Against Lovers* – Julietta only appears in five scenes, spending most of the play offstage, and her speeches are only ever a few lines long (see Davenant 1673, pp. 277, 288, 301–302, 306–308, and 326; second pagination, as well as Table 1). Certainly, Long played a series of minor characters (often maids) thereafter, in, for example, *The Cutter of Coleman Street* (Jane), *The Adventures of Five Hours* (Flora), *The Slighted Maid* (Diacelia), and *The Step-Mother* (Brianella). She was then cast in supporting roles in Sir George Etherege's *The Comical Revenge* (Mrs Rich) and *Henry the Fifth* (Queen of France), before, immediately prior to *Macbeth*, playing Leucippe (yet another maid) in *The Rivals*. Among such a list of parts, the comparatively substantial and demanding role of Lady Macduff – who has to hold her own onstage as one of the quartet of main characters – is an eyebrow-raising outlier. It is even more so, given that Long then quickly afterwards receded back into small parts: following revivals of *The Rivals* and *The Comical Revenge* over the winter of 1664–5, she added Zarma (one of Roxolana's waiting women) in *Mustapha* to her 'line' in April 1665 (*LS*, pp. 87–88). It would be highly unusual for a Restoration actor to switch lines during a season in this way; indeed, according to Elizabeth Howe (1992, pp. 75–76), Long's breakthrough role only came about in 1667 in the form of Hippolito, a comic travesty role, in Davenant and Dryden's *The Tempest, or the Enchanted Island*.

Long's roster of parts leads me to suspect that she was not the original Lady Macduff but took over the role either sometime after the theatres reopened following the Great Fire, around 1667, or even only in 1673 for the Dorset Garden revival. If we were to search for an alternative candidate for the part in 1664, on balance the evidence would point to someone like Anne Gibbs Shadwell, who, as we have seen, was developing a strong line in morally impeccable women in Lady Macduff's mould at just this moment.[26] By 1664, Gibbs Shadwell had extensive experience of working alongside the Bettertons and Harris, and while we cannot be absolutely certain that she was the first Lady Macduff, it is nevertheless likely that

[26] We do not know when Gibbs married Thomas Shadwell, but *BD* (vol. 13, p. 275) conjectures that it was around 1663–4; she only appears as Shadwell in a cast-list in 1667.

someone of her calibre within the company was responsible for it, rather than Long. Indeed, Long more plausibly played the maid with whom Lady Macduff is frequently accompanied onstage (e.g. in Act 2, scene 5, and Act 4, scene 2). This would have provided her with ample opportunity to watch how the original actress created her performance, before she took it over later; Gibbs Shadwell herself may have been in a similar situation with Mary Betterton regarding Heraclia in *The Rivals*, which the latter seems to have relinquished around 1668, as we have seen.

All this suggests that Davenant sought in *Macbeth* to balance theatrical innovation, in the form of 'diegetic supernaturalism', with his long-established formulae, including standard casting lines, for heroic plays: historically removed subject matter, with the villainous and passionate Bettertons playing in opposition to the noble and moral Harris and (probably) Anne Gibbs Shadwell. While he no doubt recognized that he needed to do things differently to compete seriously with Killigrew, Davenant nevertheless sought to do so in a way that maintained his own company's strengths as much as possible: his version of Act 4, scene 1, for example, cut the diabolical apparitions who speak the riddles to Macbeth in Shakespeare's original. These would surely have provided impressive scenic spectacle on a par with the 'Ariel-Spirits' that fly around Zempoalla in *The Indian Queen*, but Davenant shunned such opportunities for needless visual effects and instead concluded the scene with the much simpler – but no less effective – procession of kings.

The competition between the two theatre companies continued into the following seasons, despite disruption caused by the enforced closure of the playhouses due to the plague and Great Fire of London between June 1665 and October 1666. While *Macbeth* and other heroic plays such as *Henry the Fifth* continued to be popular at LIF, Killigrew made a concerted effort to build on the success of *The Indian Queen*. In 1665, he commissioned Dryden to write a sequel to his earlier play, titled *The Indian Emperour*, which cannily reused the sets and costumes from the original production, thus saving vital capital for the company. In Act 2, for example, Montezuma, like Zempoalla before him, visits a 'Magitians Cave' (2.1), where he is sung at by supernatural spirits and even confronted by the Indian Queen's ghost in a small cameo role. Davenant, keen to fight back, countered this with a production of *Mustapha* (1665), a follow up of his own play, *The Siege of Rhodes*. If Killigrew's heroic plays now emphasized his commitment to 'diegetic supernaturalism', *Mustapha* returned LIF to pre-*Macbeth* conventions: no magic, limited music, but a strong investment in scenic veracity and actors' performances. Where Killigrew was accused of frugality in reusing sets and costumes, Davenant insisted that *Mustapha* be 'new Cloath'd with new Scenes' and took 'great Care of having it perfect and exactly perform'd' (Downes 1987, p. 58). These two plays in some ways epitomized the distinctive house styles of both companies respectively; they went up directly against each other when they were both premiered in April 1665 (*LS*, p. 87).

It was only in the 1667–8 season that Shakespeare was once again a significant presence in the active repertory. Killigrew mounted one-off performances of *The Merry Wives of Windsor* on 15 August and *1 Henry IV* on 2 November 1667 (*LS*, pp. 111 and 122), as well as producing John Lacy's adaptation, *Sauny the Scot; or, The Taming of the Shrew*, the previous April (*LS*, p. 106). Lacy was a leading *farceur* of the company and wrote a number of plays that showcased his own acting talents, especially his proclivity for unusual accents and dialects (*BD*, vol. 9, p. 99). As Sauny (the equivalent of Petruchio's servant, Grumio, in Shakespeare's *Taming of the Shrew*), Lacy entertains the audience with a foul-mouthed Scottish clown who comments subversively on the actions of the main characters. At the play's conclusion, for example, when Petruchio asks Margaret (Katherine) if he can finally count on her earnest recantation – she has been testing him throughout the play, including at one point by playing dead – Sauny makes an acerbic aside to the audience: 'You ken very well she was awway's a lying Quean when she as living, and wull ye believe her now she's Dead?' (Lacy 1997, 5.1.251–3), punning on 'Quean' as slang for prostitute. Pascale Aebischer (2001, p. 27) suggests that Lacy's decision to make Sauny explicitly Scottish was prompted by his wish 'to extend his range of comic outsiders', and indeed his roster of parts does demand a level of skill with mastering non-standard accents and dialects. In addition to Sauny, for example, Lacy also played the Welshman, Lord Audley, in an undocumented production of Thomas Heywood's *The Royall King, and the Loyal Subject* (1637), as well as Teague, the Irish brogue-speaking servant, in

Sir Robert Howard's play *The Committee* (1662). He also played Frenchmen such as Ragoû in his own play, *The Old Troop* (c.1665) and Galliard in William Cavendish's *The Variety*, which was first performed in Vere Street in March 1662. As Clark (ed., 1997, p. xlviii) remarks, however, Sauny's language in *Sauny* bears considerable parallels with the Yorkshire dialect provided for Innocentia in his later comedy, *Sir Hercules Buffoon, or the Poetical Squire* (1684), belying the authenticity of his 'Scottishness'. Lacy's adaptation, then, was an attempt to advance his own acting celebrity, but it was also part of Killigrew's wider response to the inter-theatrical competition between his company and its rival, which would continue throughout the remainder of the 1667–8 season.

That competition was very much advanced by Davenant's final Shakespeare adaptation before his death in 1668. *The Tempest, or the Enchanted Island* was produced in November 1667. It enjoyed an initial run of seven days and was regularly revived thereafter (*LS*, pp. 123–124 and *passim*), being further adapted into a full-scale dramatic opera by Thomas Shadwell for Dorset Garden in 1674; this operatic version held the stage until the nineteenth century (Spencer 1965). The composition and production of the play at LIF neatly demonstrate how material and institutional contexts such as the availability of personnel or the state of the commercial competition with Killigrew's theatre could impact the ways in which a text was adapted. In particular, three factors determined how *The Tempest* entered the repertory in the winter of 1667–8: first, collaborative authorship; second, a new fashion for cross-dressing roles, and third, Betterton's prolonged absence from the stage during this period.

Unusually for Davenant, he chose to adapt *The Tempest* in collaboration with the rising star of the Restoration theatre: John Dryden. This fact is remarkable for a number of reasons. For a start, it represents the earliest instance in the post-1660 theatre of two professional playwrights working together on a script. The majority of (the very few) collaborations in this period tended to be the products of 'genteel amateurs writing either with each other or with professionals' (Kewes 1998, p. 135). Men like George Villiers, the Duke of Buckingham (*The Rehearsal*, 1671), William Cavendish, the Duke of Newcastle (*The Country Gentleman*, 1669), John Wilmot, the Earl of Rochester (*Valentinian*, 1685), or Sir Robert Howard would team up with friends and family or work with an established playwright to ready their scripts for performance. We have already seen, for example, that a group of wits translated *Pompey the Great* in 1664. But as Kewes (1998, pp. 154–155) notes, 'Of the more than 400 plays written in the half-century following the Stuart Restoration, only two were products of a professional partnership': *Oedipus* (1678) and *The Duke of Guise* (1682), both by Dryden in collaboration with Nathaniel Lee. Changing ideas about authorship, originality, and literary property meant that the kinds of collaborative models that dominated the pre-1642 playwrighting industry were wholly unsuitable after the Restoration (Rosenthal 1996; Kewes 1998). It is a remarkable but under-appreciated fact, therefore, that Dryden was the most frequent professional collaborator between 1660 and 1700. However, even Kewes neglects to incorporate Dryden's much earlier partnership with Davenant into her otherwise astute analysis (no doubt because theirs was an adaptation of an existing text rather than an original work). It is important to do so, however, if we are to understand why the play was selected for production in 1667.

As we have seen, Davenant's box office had been hurt by Killigrew's promotion of 'diegetic supernaturalism', and so he sought to counter this with his *Macbeth*. Dryden was central to this new theatrical mode, and his plays were generally becoming increasingly popular with audiences. Up until August 1667, he had worked exclusively with the King's Company but suddenly, for reasons which remain obscure, in that month his play, *The Feigned Innocence, or Sir Martin Mar-All*, was produced by Davenant at LIF (*LS*, p. 111). Winn (1987, p. 181) puts this shift from Killigrew to Davenant's company down to politics and Dryden's support for the Yorkist faction at court. It is certainly true that the Duke of York was LIF's patron, but surely more local, theatrical, considerations played a part in the move too; Miyoshi (2012, p. 29) thinks that intra-theatrical politics were involved: Davenant, 'seeing that the veteran players of Killigrew's troupe were causing mayhem at the other house, opportunistically decided to deal a deathblow to his competitor'. The mayhem referred to here concerned bitter squabbles between the King's Company's leading actors, Charles Hart and Michael Mohun, as well as its unprofessional actresses, who, differing in their approaches to rehearsal, 'fell out and called each other whores' (Pepys 1995, vol. 8, p. 503).

It would appear, then, that Davenant had come to some kind of arrangement with Dryden in an attempt to lure him away from Bridges Street to work instead with the Duke's Company. In his preface to the 1670 edition of *The Tempest*, Dryden acknowledged Davenant's positive influence on him, both as a lover of Shakespeare and as a developing playwright. It is worth quoting the preface at length. Explaining that *The Tempest* was originally by Shakespeare, Dryden goes on to assert that this was

> *a Poet for whom he* [Davenant] *had particularly a high veneration, and who he first taught me to admire. The Play it self had formerly been acted with success at the* Black-Fryers: *and our excellent* Fletcher *had so great a value for it, that he thought fit to make use of the same Design, not much varied, a second time. Those who have seen his Sea-Voyage, may easily discern that it was a Copy of* Shakespear's Tempest: *the Storm, the desart Island, and the Woman who had never seen a Man, are all sufficient testimonies of it* [. . .] *Sir William D'avenant, as he was a man of quick and piercing imagination, soon found that somewhat might be added to the Design of* Shakespear [. . .] *and therefore to put the last hand to it, he design'd the Counterpart to* Shakespear's *Plot, namely that of a Man who had never seen a Women, that by this means those two Characters of Innocence and Love might the more illustrate and commend each other. This excellent contrivance he was pleas'd to communicate to me, and to desire my assistance in it. I confess that from the very first moment it so pleas'd me, that I never writ any thing with more delight. I must likewise do him that justice to acknowledge, that my writing received daily his amendments, and that is the reason why it is not so faulty, as the rest which I have done without the help or correction of so judicious a friend.*
>
> (Davenant and Dryden 1997, pp. 83–84)

Dryden's comments reveal both the motivation for adapting *The Tempest* at this specific moment and the process of doing so. Now that Dryden was working for Davenant, the manager could use his talents to his advantage. Davenant gave

Dryden the plot outline to the most radical element of the new text: in the adaptation, the courtship between Miranda and Ferdinand is mirrored by the introduction of her younger sister, Dorinda, and the '*Man who had never seen a Women*', Hippolito, who has been brought up in isolation in a cave by Prospero but is, in fact, the rightful heir to the Dukedom of Mantua. It was Dryden's responsibility to flesh out these scenes with witty dialogue, under Davenant's instruction (Watkins 2023a, pp. 19–20). Davenant, we are told, wrote '*The Comical parts of the Saylors*' himself (Davenant and Dryden 1997, p. 84).

The resulting play was a comic pastiche on the heroic love-and-honour motifs of earlier LIF productions such as *Rhodes* and *Henry the Fifth*. Moreover, it also took a humorous approach to the supernatural spectacle associated with plays like *The Indian Queen* and *Macbeth*. Not only does it retain the character of the magical Ariel, who sings and dances throughout the course of the play, spectators would have been treated to a lavish storm scene in Act 1, scene 1, depicted in perspective scenes and accompanied by music. (Of course, Ariel does not fly at LIF, as they would do at Dorset Garden in 1674: Shadwell's script includes directions such as 'Ariel *speaks, hovering in the Air*' [Spencer, ed., 1965, 5.2.36SD].) Moreover, Davenant and Dryden incorporated another opportunity for 'diegetic supernaturalism' in the form of the Masque of Devils in Act 2, scene 1. Here the Italians, Alonzo, Antonio, and Gonzalo, witness a pair of devils singing a song on the themes of usurpation, ambition, and overthrowing legitimate kings, in the same vein as the witches' songs in *Macbeth*:

1.	Devil	*Where does proud* Ambition *dwell?*
2.	Devil	*In the lowest Rooms of Hell.*
1.	Devil	*Of the damn'd who leads the Host?*
2.	Devil	*He who did oppress the most.*
1.	Devil	*Who such Troops of damned brings*
2.	Devil	*Most are led by fighting Kings.*
		King who did Crowns unjustly get,
		Here on burning Thrones are set.

(2.1.47–54)

Thus, the mortal characters are once again confronted by otherworldly spirits. The innocent Gonzalo asks, in an echo of Lady Macduff, 'Do evil Spirits imitate the good, | In showing men their sins?' (2.1.58).

The Tempest does not simply rework the 'diegetic supernaturalism' of *Macbeth*, however. It also responds to, and builds on, other plays in the wider repertory. Most immediately, Davenant appears to have produced *The Tempest* to counter the King's Company's production of Fletcher's *The Sea Voyage* – retitled *The Storm* – as Dryden notes in his preface. This was premiered at the very beginning of the new season, on 25 September with patronage from the royal court; Pepys observed how the auditorium was 'infinitely full, the King and all the Court almost there'. The actual performance was, according to Pepys, 'but so so', but it was saved by an addition to the original text: 'a most admirable dance at the end, of the ladies in a Military manner, which endeed did please me mightily' (1995, vol. 8, p. 450). Fletcher's play was certainly inspired by Shakespeare's text, and Dryden, in a later essay, argued that while 'Shakespear *is generally worth our Imitation* [. . .] *to imitate* Fletcher *is but to Copy after him who was a Copyer*' (1956–2002, vol. 13, p. 240). In other words, Fletcher is two removes from Shakespearean source, and so Davenant may here have intended to counter Killigrew by staging the real thing, albeit in altered form. This kind of thinking found a precedent in the staging of his rewritten *Macbeth* in response to *The Indian Queen*, which directly imitated Shakespeare's text in Act 3, scene 2, as we have seen. The performance of *The Tempest* in November 1667 made comparison with *The Storm* explicit in its prologue, such that audiences would have been aware of the rivalry between the two shows:

> *The Storm which vanish'd on the Neighb'ring shore,*
> *Was taught by* Shakespear'*s Tempest first to roar.*
> *That innocence and beauty which did smile*
> *In* Fletcher, *grew on this Enchanted Isle.*
> *But* Shakespear'*s Magick could not copy'd be,*
> *Within that Circle none durst walk but he.*
>
> (Davenant and Dryden 1997, p. 87)

While it may well look as though Davenant intended to go head-to-head with *The Storm*, in fact both plays are part of a larger pattern, which goes back to at least February 1667, when Killigrew revived Sir John Suckling's comedy, *The Goblins* (1646), which Dryden also namechecks as an imitation of *The Tempest*, noting that Suckling's character, Reginella, is '*an open imitation of* Shakespear's *Miranda*' (Davenant and Dryden 1997, pp. 83–84). All these plays make a significant investment in dancing, as Miyoshi (2012, p. 29) points out – the women's military dance at the end of *The Storm* balanced by the 'Seamans dance' (Pepys 1995, vol. 9, p. 48), which probably occurred in Act 2, scene 3 of *The Tempest*, as well as Ariel and Milcha's *Saraband* (5.2.26sd), which concluded it. More importantly, however, all these plays indulge the desire to have actors and especially actresses cross dress in their roles.

Beth H. Friedman-Rommel (1995, p. 464) has observed that female cross-dressing in the Restoration theatre falls into two categories: breeches parts, in which a female character 'assumes male disguise as part of the narrative structure of the play', and travesty roles, where an actress takes on a male role for the duration of the play. Breeches parts and travesty roles were extremely popular in the Restoration repertory, with around a quarter of plays produced between 1660 and 1700 calling for at least one cross-dressed woman's part (Wilson, 1958). Dryden himself had included breeches roles in *The Rival Ladies* (1664), when two women disguise themselves as pages in order to pursue the man they love. In March 1667, Pepys recorded seeing Moll Davis 'dance in boy's clothes' at the end of *The English Princess*, before comparing this unfavourably to Nell Gwynn's 'dancing the other day at the King's house in boy's clothes' (1995, vol. 8, p. 101).

The Tempest thus took advantage of this phenomenon in the form of the newly introduced character, Hippolito, to compete with Killigrew's repertory. The prologue to the play suggests that, owing to a lack of male performers, the theatre was '*forc'd t'employ | One of our Women to present a Boy*' (Davenant and Dryden 1997, p. 87). The part was very likely played by Jane Long in what must have been a breakthrough role – one of the first major speaking parts of her career. Indeed, during the 1666–7 season, she had been developing a new line in breeches parts. She played Dulcino in

James Shirley's *The Grateful Servant* (1629) in c.1667, 'the first time', Downes (1987, p. 60) observes, 'she appear'd in Man's Habit'. She would go on to play the title role in Betterton's own *The Woman Made a Justice* (1670; now lost), which we can presume also saw the heroine disguise herself as a judge (*LS*, p. 168; Howe 1992, pp. 75–76). But unlike these other roles, Hippolito is, strictly speaking, a travesty part, rather than a breeches role: the character is gendered male but played by an actress: we are told explicitly not to '*expect in the last Act to find | Her Sex transform'd from man to Woman-kind*' (Davenant and Dryden 1997, p. 87). Whether or not we can read the prologue sincerely or ironically (was Davenant really '*forc'd t'employ*' a woman instead of a man?), he nevertheless got creative mileage out of the result. Davenant and Dryden adapted *The Tempest* in full knowledge that Long would take the role – regardless of whether this was something they chose or was something forced upon them. The penchant for cross-dressing evidenced in other plays in the repertory at this time would have made the casting choice a viable commercial option either way.

It is certainly plausible that necessity was the mother of invention in this instance. No full roster for the 1667–8 season survives, but the number of male parts required by the play does seem to exceed the number of available actors that can be verified as present in the company. This leads us to another major issue related to casting that affected the ways in which *The Tempest* was adapted: between October 1667 and June 1668, Thomas Betterton fell ill and was unable to perform. Although Davenant may have initially intended him for Prospero, Betterton is not recorded as ever having performed in the play (Milhous 1975). A major strand of criticism has explored the fact that the Restoration Prospero is a much reduced figure from Shakespeare's patriarch: he lacks the former's authority, judgement, and power (Spencer 1927, p. 203; Eisaman Maus 1982; Auberlen 1991; Wikander 1991). This may be due to the fact that Betterton, the expert in overbearing rant, was not available to play it.

Betterton's absence had a profound impact on the repertory of the subsequent season and prompts us to question how the play would have been cast for performance. Davenant appears to have continued to build on the known lines of the other company actors at the same time that he offers others (like Long) the opportunity to pursue new creative directions. We can infer, for example, that Prospero would have been taken by an actor such as John Young, who had already taken over as Macbeth on 16 October 1667 and who was still in that role the day before *The Tempest*'s premiere (*LS*, pp. 120, 123). We know from external sources that Edward Angel, having recently joined LIF, played Stephano, while the company's beloved comedian, Cave Underhill, took Trincalo (see *LS*, p. 123), which makes perfect sense, given his skill in physical comedy and his unattractive physique. We can surmise too that Samuel Sandford, fresh from playing Hecate, would have taken on Sycorax, Caliban's incestuous sister, in what was very likely another travesty role, given his aptitude with these sorts of comic grotesques. In 1708, Richard Cross (*fl.* 1695–1725) played both Sycorax and one of the witches in *Macbeth* (*BD*, vol. 4, p. 66; on these male-to-female travesty roles, see Ritchie 2023). Perhaps James Nokes, another stalwart company comedian, played alongside Sandford as Caliban.

We know Harris played Ferdinand, because he is noted as having sung the celebrated echo duet 'Go thy way' alongside Ariel in Act 3, scene 4. Ariel was most likely played by the musical Moll Davis – the character is not only required to dance, as we have seen, but also called upon to underscore the duet with a guitar, an instrument on which Davis was proficient (see *BD*, vol. 4, p. 224). Unfortunately, we have no evidence for who played Miranda and Dorinda, but they may have been taken by either of the two leading actresses in the company at this time, Mary Betterton and Anne Gibbs Shadwell. Certainly, this casting would make sense, given both actresses' history of playing Harris's onstage lovers. Alternatively, one of these parts might have been filled by a Mrs. Jennings, a longstanding but rather junior member of the Duke's Company, who was only beginning to be offered main roles in this season: her first major part for which we have evidence was Ariana in Etherege's *She Would If She Could*, performed three months after *The Tempest* premiere, on 6 February 1668 (*LS*, p. 129; see also *BD*, vol. 8, p. 154). She became known for her line in virtuous young women in love with the comic gallant, which speaks nicely to the two girls in *The Tempest*, particularly Dorinda. It would be perfectly plausible to envisage Harris and Mary Betterton as Ferdinand and Miranda with Long and Jennings as

Hippolito and Dorinda. Winifred Gosnell had returned to the company sometime in 1666, and given that she inherited the role of Ariel after Davis's retirement from the stage in 1668 – Pepys (1995, vol. 9, p. 422) recorded that the performance on 21 January 1669 was 'but ill done, by Gosnell in lieu of Mall Davis' – she likely played Milcha, Ariel's dancing companion, in the initial run.

It we turn to another production from the LIF repertory in the 1667–8 season, we can see how the absence of Betterton might have freed up the ways in which Davenant envisaged his Shakespeare adaptation. The next new play premiered at LIF after *The Tempest* was Sir George Etherege's second comedy, *She Would If She Could* on 6 February 1668 (*LS*, p. 129). Much anticipated, the play suffered badly in performance, evidently because the company were under-rehearsed (Cordner 1994). What is important for our purposes, however, is that Etherege's play too seems to have been written with Betterton's absence in mind. Indeed, from what we know of its casting, it would appear that Mary Betterton had also been unavailable, probably because she was caring for her husband for a time, prompting us to question whether or not she was involved in the earlier Shakespeare production as well. If we look at the parts for which we have information about performers, we can see that there were no obvious roles for them to take up on their return:

Sir Oliver Cockwood	James Nokes
Sir Joslyn Jolly	Henry Harris
Courtall	William Smith
Freeman	John Young
Lady Cockwood	Anne Gibbs Shadwell
Ariana	Mrs Jennings
Gatty	Moll Davis

All the remaining parts – such as Rakehell – are minor roles and would not be suitable for either Betterton. Perhaps it was the case, then, that Davenant was using the Bettertons' absence from the stage in order to write and commission works for different configurations of actors, thereby expanding on the formulas he had developed since 1661.[27]

The desire for more cross-dressed characters and the absence of the Bettertons during the season meant that Davenant had an opportunity to showcase new talent in his company, promoting actresses like Long and Jennings, who had hitherto played bit parts but who were now able to take on more demanding roles. By removing, albeit temporarily, the giant redwood of a Betterton meant that the younger plants could find the light and air to grow. *The Tempest*, like *She Would*, resulted in part from this process. Unlike Davenant's other adaptations, *The Tempest* is not blindly restricted to the heroic structures of *Law Against Lovers*, *The Rivals*, or *Macbeth*. These plays had to find a prominent position for Betterton, often in opposition to Harris. His absence meant that Davenant could afford to reduce Prospero's role (rather than building up another part to work alongside it) and redistribute the rest of the play among the younger actresses and the comedians – the sailors are a major attraction of the piece, as Pepys's comments about their dance suggests. As such, *The Tempest* takes advantage of what he had learnt from the wider repertory – Dryden's 'diegetic supernaturalism', for example – while continuing to explore new avenues and formulas, particularly in terms of comedy. Indeed, there seems to have been a focus in these years on promoting young members of both companies: Pepys frequently visited the apprentice actors at Killigrew's recently established 'nursery' in the 1667–8 season, and he recorded attending a performance of *The Marriage Night* at LIF on 21 March 1667, where 'only the young men and women of the house Act' (1995, vol. 8, p. 122).

[27] The connections between *She Would If She Could* and *The Tempest* are closer than it might at first appear. One character reports of the rakish Sir Oliver Cockwood (Nokes) that 'there is not such another wild man in the town; all his talk was of wenching, and swearing, and drinking, and tearing' (Etherege 1982, 1.2.47–9). This reverses Prospero's warning to his daughters that 'the danger lies in a wild | Young man' who 'run[s] wild about the Woods' (Davenant and Dryden 1997, 2.4.104–6). Later, Gatty (Davis) and Ariana (Jennings) are shocked by the appearance of Courtall and Freeman hiding in a closet: 'We are almost scared out of our wits', she explains to the Cockwoods, 'my sister went to reach my guitar out of the closet, and found 'em both shut up there' (5.1.383–5); Gatty was played by Davis, who also played the guitar as Ariel.

6 Conclusion

Davenant died on 7 April 1668, bringing an abrupt end to the often intense but highly creative and (mostly) good-natured competition with Killigrew. In a back-handed tribute to his memory, another of Davenant's early rivals, Richard Flecknoe, hastily printed what he called a 'poetical fiction': *Sr William D'avenant's Voyage to the Other World: With His Adventures in the Poets Elizium* (1668). This was a caustic final jibe at the poet laureate. In the text, Davenant is shown, Dante-like, descending down to the 'Poets Elyzium' (p. 7), where he finds the chief authors of both ancient and modern times: Homer, Virgil, Tasso, Spenser, and Jonson. On meeting them, however, Davenant is 'amaz'd' to discover that they each refuse to welcome him among their ranks for the awkward fact that, in life, he had 'disoblig'd' each of them by his 'discommendations' of their worth. (Indeed, Davenant had done so in the preface to *Gondibert*.) Disgruntled and embarrassed, he quickly passes on to Shakespeare, 'whom he thought to have found his greatest Friend' (p. 8). But, of course, this turns into yet another humiliating encounter: Shakespeare too 'was as much offended with him as any of the rest, for so spoiling and mangling of his Plays' (p. 8). As a result, Davenant is banished from the poets' company, 'condemned' instead 'to live in Pluto's Court', where he will make the god and his consort, Proserpina, eternally 'merry with his facetious Jeasts and Stories' (p. 11). The message is simple: as a result of his hubris and precocious self-promotion, and lack of respect for his predecessors while alive in this world, Davenant has forfeited the consoling company of his fellow poets to become a mercenary hanger-on of yet another decadent court. '[H]e is now in as good Condition as he was before', Flecknoe concludes, 'and lives the same Life there, as he did here' (p. 13).

Flecknoe's final assessment of Davenant – that he so spoiled and mangled Shakespeare's plays that he should be consigned to hell – has found its corollary in a particular strand of twentieth-century scholarship. It is not too far, as we have seen, from Hazelton Spencer (1927, pp. 201–202), who, writing about Davenant and Dryden's *The Tempest*, concluded that 'To appraise this wretched stuff in the light of the critical rules would be absurd [. . .] it is *mangled*' (my emphasis). Such critics place undue stress on the ways in which Shakespeare's texts were altered as pieces of writing without considering the very practical and defensible theatrical and material reasons for adaptation. On the other hand, of course, we have Dryden's appraisal of Davenant as '*a man of quick and piercing imagination*', who venerated Shakespeare and who lovingly adapted the scripts in order to ensure that they remained viable as living performance vehicles:

> *As when a Tree's cut down the secret root*
> *Lives under ground, and thence new Branches shoot;*
> *So, for old* Shakespear's *honour'd dust, this day*
> *Springs up and buds a new reviving Play*
>
> (Davenant and Dryden 1997, p. 87)

This tradition has found much more sympathy in the twenty-first century when scholars have at last tried to take the adaptations on their own terms. This might involve excavating their engagement with contemporary politics or with exploring how they make use of new theatre technologies and conventions, such as moveable scenery, music, or women performers. It also incorporates those investigations into how Shakespeare was being constructed as a 'national poet' during the later seventeenth century, through both exposure in the theatre, through print, and in the emerging forms of literary criticism. As a result of all these approaches, we are much better informed about the motivations lying behind Shakespeare adaptation in the Restoration period.

This Element has sought to address a slightly different question, however. I have tried to demonstrate that we can only understand Davenant's approach to adaptation if we attend to what else was being staged at LIF at the same time. Theatre makers in the Restoration were as much driven by economic motives as they were by aesthetic or political concerns; indeed, these frequently overlapped. It stands to reason, then, that Davenant would adapt existing texts to maximize his profits. Certainly, this might mean indulging audiences' desires for music and spectacle or appealing to the racier political debates and scandals of the day. But it also meant providing his actors with parts that fit snuggly into their established lines so that they could rehearse and perform them as effectively as possible, drawing on known generic conventions. Only in this way could the Duke's Company remain agile enough to respond quickly and flexibly to anything their competitors at the King's Company might throw at them.

Through an analysis of Davenant's Shakespeare plays in the context of LIF's wider repertory we can see more clearly why they were adapted in the ways that they were. By setting *The Law Against Lovers* alongside *The Siege of Rhodes*, for example, we can tentatively chart the establishment of particular 'lines' that Davenant's young and inexperienced company of actors would take up and develop in future works. While my suggestions for individual roles in the adaptation must, in the end, remain purely speculative, it is by thinking about the plays from a casting perspective, we can see how Davenant built the play on the same character types and relational structures of the earlier play. Similarly, by placing Davenant's production of *Henry VIII* and *The Rivals* in the context of other heroic plays from the period, such as Orrery's *Henry the Fifth*, we begin to discern the emergence of a particular 'house style', typified in this case by verisimilar scenography and costumes, historical settings, and set-piece dances and pageants. Having identified this 'house style', we are now in a position to explore variations within it – with Stapleton's *The Step-Mother*, for instance – tracking the development of Davenant's legacy beyond his own career. We are also in a position to ask whether Killigrew's company curated a similarly self-conscious and distinctive house style through its repertory decisions, and whether or not this responded to competition from LIF beyond the years of the Davenant-Killigrew rivalry.

Indeed, *Shakespeare and the Restoration Repertory* offers evidence that Davenant was not, in fact, always the leading theatrical innovator of the two patent managers, with Killigrew persistently trailing behind, as scholars such as Judith Milhous, Mary Edmond, and Dawn Lewcock have suggested. Instead, we have seen that, with the opening of his new theatre in Bridges Street in 1663, Killigrew began to corner the market in a new form of what Walkling terms spectacle-tragedy, characterized by its scenes of 'diegetic supernaturalism'. The popularity of *The Indian Queen*, I have argued, forced Davenant's hand as he prepared his next season; he had to temporarily abandon LIF house style and provide a spectacle-tragedy of his own in the form of *Macbeth*. Even as that play continued to operate within the logic of LIF's other repertory staples in terms of casting, it nevertheless underscored the precarity of Davenant's theatrical enterprise. This precarity was even more in evidence when it came to staging *The Tempest* in 1667, after months of disruption due to plague and the Great Fire. By this time, Davenant had managed to secure the talents of Dryden, one of Killigrew's most bankable writers, in an effort to depress Bridges Street's box office. But this was quickly undermined by the (temporary) loss of Betterton to illness. Betterton's prolonged absence from the stage meant that the usual casting model of LIF plays needed to be immediately reconfigured. This presented Davenant with an opportunity to showcase the talents of some of the more junior, non-sharer members in the company, such as Moll Davis and Jane Long. The recent trend for cross-dressed performances, as seen in other plays like *The Grateful Servant*, encouraged Davenant and Dryden to place these young performers front-and-centre in erotically charged and highly demanding roles. *The Tempest*, along like *She Would If She Could*, was written and produced at an important if unsettled juncture in the history of Duke's Company, when older dramaturgical models were no longer viable. As such, Davenant used both plays to scout out potential new directions of travel for the company at the same time that he gave his future star actresses their big breaks.

What does this all mean for future discussions of Restoration Shakespeare? The arbitrary distinction between 'Old Stock Plays' (Downes 1987, p. 24) and new, post-1660 works was one that the Restoration theatre managers certainly recognized. However, they did so only in their legal wrangling over which plays they were entitled to inherit following the establishment of their respective patent companies. In terms of the active repertory such niceties were next to useless: plays were either successful, and therefore retained for future revival, or they were not. As such, to talk about the 'Shakespearean repertory' or even the pre-1642 repertory within a Restoration theatre context makes absurdly little sense (Sorelius 1966; Hume 2004). Much more important was whether or not the old stock looked and sounded vibrant and *new* – whether it could hold its own – as it jostled for attention next to the latest heroic drama or sex comedy. Davenant thus pursued an approach that ensured Shakespeare remained always *à la mode* rather than *démodé*. To do so, he looked around to what else was playing, both at home at LIF and abroad at Bridges Street.

By adding new characters, rearranging scenes, adjusting dialogue, and incorporating musical and scenic spectacle in ways familiar from other plays in the repertory, Davenant could rely on his actors to understand what was required of them to generate a satisfying and successful performance. Moreover, he ensured that his audiences would appreciate those performances because they too had a working knowledge of the generic conventions, acting 'lines', and scenic structures that determined any particular production at LIF. In order to comprehend fully what a performance of Shakespeare meant in the first decade of the Restoration, it is imperative that we set that performance within the broader context of its surrounding repertory.

References

Aebischer, Pascale. '"Steal[ing] out o' th' old plays" in John Lacy's *Sauny the Scott: Or, the Taming of the Shrew*'. *Restoration & Eighteenth-Century Theatre Research*, vol. 16, no. 1, 2001, pp. 24–41.

Auberlen, Eckhard. '*The Tempest* and the Concerns of the Restoration Court: A Study of *The Enchanted Island* and the Operatic *Tempest*'. *Restoration*, vol. 15, no. 2, 1991, pp. 71–88.

Bartholomeusz, Dennis. *Macbeth and the Players*. Cambridge: Cambridge University Press, 1969.

Behn, Aphra. *Oroonoko*, edited by Joanna Lipking. New York: W. W. Norton, 1997.

Boyle, Roger. *The Dramatic Works of Roger Boyle, Earl of Orrery*, edited by William Smith Clark II. 2 vols. Cambridge, MA: Harvard University Press, 1937. [Orrery 1937]

Carlson, Marvin. *The Haunted Stage: The Theatre as Memory Machine*. Ann Abor: The University of Michigan Press, 2001.

Cibber, Colley. *An Apology for the Life of Mr Colley Cibber, Comedian and Late Patentee of the Theatre Royal: A Modernized Text*, edited by David Roberts. Cambridge: Cambridge University Press, 2022.

Clark, Sandra, ed. *Shakespeare Made Fit: Restoration Adaptations of Shakespeare*. London: Everyman, 1997.

Cordner, Michael. 'Etherege's *She Would if She Could*: Comedy, Complaisance and Anti-climax'. In *English Comedy*, edited by Michael Cordner, Peter Holland, and John Kerrigan. Cambridge: Cambridge University Press, 1994, pp. 158–179.

Crowne, John. *The Misery of Civil-War*. London, 1680.

Davenant, William. *The Rivals: A Comedy*. London, 1668.

The Works of Sr William Davenant K^t. London, 1673.

Macbeth, a Tragœdy: With all the Alterations, Amendments, Additions, and New Songs. London, 1674.

Gondibert, edited by David F. Gladish. Oxford: Clarendon Press, 1971.

The Siege of Rhodes: A Critical Edition, edited by Ann-Mari Hedbäck. Studia Anglistica Upsaliensia 14. Uppsala: Acta Universitatis Upsaliensis, 1973.

Davenant, William, and John Dryden. *The Tempest, or the Enchanted Island. Shakespeare Made Fit: Restoration Adaptations of Shakespeare*, edited by Sandra Clark. London: Everyman, 1997, pp. 79–185.

Dent, Edward J. *Foundations of English Opera: A Study in Musical Drama in English during the Seventeenth Century*. Cambridge: Cambridge University Press, 1928.

Depledge, Emma. *Shakespeare's Rise to Cultural Prominence: Politics, Print and Alteration, 1642–1700*. Cambridge: Cambridge University Press, 2018.

Dobson, Michael. *The Making of the National Poet: Shakespeare, Adaptation, and Authorship, 1660–1769*. Oxford: Clarendon Press, 1992.

Downes, John. *Roscius Anglicanus*, edited by Judith Milhous, and Robert D. Hume. London: The Society for Theatre Research, 1987.

Dryden, John. *The Works of John Dryden*, edited by Hugh Thomas Swedenberg Jr., Edward Niles Hooker, Vinton A. Dearing et al. 20 vols. Berkeley: University of California Press, 1956–2002.

Edmond, Mary. *Rare Sir William Davenant: Poet Laureate, Playwright, Civil War General, Restoration Theatre Manager*. Manchester: Manchester University Press, 1987.

Eisaman Maus, Katharine. 'Arcadia Lost: Politics and Revision in the Restoration *Tempest*'. *Renaissance Drama*, vol. 13, 1982, pp. 189–209.

Etherege, George. *The Plays of Sir George Etherege*, edited by Michael Cordner. Cambridge: Cambridge University Press, 1982.

Eubanks Winkler, Amanda. ed. *Music for 'Macbeth'*. Middleton, WI: A-R Editions, 2004.

⸺ *O Let Us Howle Some Heavy Note: Music for Witches, the Melancholic, and the Mad on the Seventeenth-Century English Stage*. Bloomington: Indiana University Press, 2006.

⸺ 'The Intermedial Dramaturgy of Dramatick Opera: Understanding Genre through Performance'. *Restoration: Studies in English Literary Culture, 1660–1700*, vol. 42, no. 2, 2018, pp. 13–38.

⸺ 'Staging Davenant; or *Macbeth* the Musical'. In *Literature and the Arts: Interdisciplinary Essays in Memory of James Anderson Winn*, edited by Anna Battigelli. Newark: University of Delaware Press, 2023, pp. 31–46.

Eubanks Winkler, Amanda, and Richard Schoch. *Shakespeare in the Theatre: Sir William Davenant and the Duke's Company*. London: Bloomsbury, 2022.

Eubanks Winkler, Amanda, Claude Fretz, and Richard Schoch, eds. *Performing Restoration Shakespeare*. Cambridge: Cambridge University Press, 2023.

Flecknoe, Richard. *Sr William D'avenant's Voyage to the Other World: With His Adventures in the Poets Eliẓium*. London, 1668.

Freehafer, Jonathan. 'The Formation of the London Patent Companies in 1660'. *Theatre Notebook*, vol. 20, 1965, pp. 6–30.

Fretz, Claude. 'Performing Restoration Shakespeare "Then" and "Now": A Case Study of Davenant's *Macbeth*'. *Concentric: Literary and Cultural Studies*, vol. 48, no. 1, 2022, pp. 27–56.

Friedman-Rommel, Beth H. 'Breaking the Code: Toward a Reception Theory of Theatrical Cross-Dressing in Eighteenth-Century London'. *Theatre Journal*, vol. 47, no. 4, 1995, pp. 459–479.

Furness, Horace Howard, ed. *A New Variorum Edition of Shakespeare: The Tempest*. 11th ed. Philadelphia: J. B. Lippincott, 1892.

Gellert, James. 'Sir William Davenant's *The Law against Lovers*: Shakespeare's Problem Comedy and the Restoration Heroic Tradition'. *Cahiers Élisabéthains*, vol. 16, no. 1, 1979, pp. 27–43.

Greenfield, Anne. 'D'Avenant's Lady Macduff: Ideal Femininity and Subversive Politics'. *Restoration*, vol. 37, no. 1, 2013, pp. 39–60.

Harbage, Alfred. *Sir William Davenant: Poet Venturer, 1606–1668*. Philadelphia: University of Pennsylvania Press, 1935.

Highfill Jr., Philip H., Kalman A. Burnim, and Edward Langhans, eds. *A Biographical Dictionary of Actors, Actresses, Musicians, Dancers, Managers & Other Stage Personnel in London, 1660–1800*. 16 vols. Carbondale and Edwardsville: Southern Illinois University Press, 1973–93. [*BD*]

Holland, Peter. *The Ornament of Action: Text and Performance in Restoration Comedy*. Cambridge: Cambridge University Press, 1979.

Hotson, Leslie. *The Commonwealth and Restoration Stage*. Cambridge, MA: Harvard University Press, 1928.

Howe, Elizabeth. *The First English Actresses: Women and Drama, 1660–1700*. Cambridge: Cambridge University Press, 1992.

Hubbard, Caitlin. 'More to Spectacle than Meets the Eye: William Davenant and the Pedagogical Power of Theatrical Spectacle'. *Restoration*, vol. 48, no. 1, 2024, pp. 49–83.

Hume, Robert D. *The Development of English Drama in the Late Seventeenth Century*. Oxford: Clarendon Press, 1976.

— 'Securing a Repertory: Plays on the London Stage, 1660–5'. In *Poetry and Drama, 1570–1700: Essays in Honour of Harold F. Brooks*, edited by Antony Coleman, and Antony Hammond. London: Methuen, 1981, pp. 156–172.

— 'Theatres and Repertory'. *The Cambridge History of British Theatre: Volume 2, 1660–1895*, edited by Joseph Donohue. Cambridge: Cambridge University Press, 2004, pp. 53–70.

Keenan, Tim. 'Adapting the Adaptors: Staging Davenant and Dryden's Restoration *Tempest*'. *Journal of Adaptation in Film & Performance*, vol. 2, no. 1, 2009, pp. 65–77.

Restoration Staging, 1660–74. Abingdon: Routledge, 2017.

Kewes, Paulina. *Authorship and Appropriation: Writing for the Stage in England, 1660–1710*. Oxford: Clarendon Press, 1998.

Klein Maguire, Nancy. *Regicide and Restoration: English Tragicomedy, 1660–1671*. Cambridge: Cambridge University Press, 1992.

Knutson, Roslyn Lander. *The Repertory of Shakespeare's Company, 1594–1613*. Fayetteville: The University of Arkansas Press, 1991.

Kroll, Richard. *Restoration Drama and 'The Circle of Commerce': Tragicomedy, Politics, and Trade in the Seventeenth Century*. Cambridge: Cambridge University Press, 2007.

Lacy, John. '*Sauny the Scot*'. In *Shakespeare Made Fit: Restoration Adaptations of Shakespeare*, edited by Sandra Clark. London: Everyman, 1997, pp. 3–78.

Langhans, Edward A. 'The Theatres'. In *The London Theatre World, 1660–1800*, edited Robert D. Hume. Carbondale and Edwardsville: Southern Illinois University Press, 1980, pp. 35–65.

'Conjectural Reconstructions of the Vere Street and Lincoln's Inn Field's Theatres'. *Essays in Theatre*, vol. 1, no. 1, 1982, pp. 14–23.

Leacroft, Richard. *The Development of the English Playhouse: An Illustrated Survey of Theatre Building in England from Medieval to Modern Times*. London: Methuen, 1973.

Lewcock, Dawn. *Sir William Davenant, the Court Masque, and the English Seventeenth-Century Scenic Stage, c. 1605–c. 1700*. Amherst, NY: Cambria Press, 2008.

Marsden, Jean I. *The Re-imagined Text: Shakespeare, Adaptation, & Eighteenth-Century Literary Theory*. Lexington: University Press of Kentucky, 1995.

McMillan, Scott and Sally-Beth MacLean. *The Queen's Men and Their Plays*. Cambridge: Cambridge University Press, 1998.

Milhous, Judith. 'An Annotated Census of Thomas Betterton's Roles, 1659–1710: Part 1'. *Theatre Notebook*, vol. 29, no. 1, 1975, pp. 33–43.

— *Thomas Betterton and the Management of Lincoln's Inn Fields, 1695–1708*. Carbondale and Edwardsville: Southern Illinois University Press, 1979.

Milhous, Judith, and Robert D. Hume, eds. *A Register of English Theatrical Documents, 1660–1737*. 2 vols. Carbondale and Edwardsville: Southern Illinois University Press, 1991.

Miller, Ted H. 'The Two Deaths of Lady Macduff: Antimetaphysics, Violence, and William Davenant's Restoration Revision of *Macbeth*'. *Political Theory*, vol. 36, no. 3, 2008, pp. 856–882.

Miyoshi, Riki. 'Thomas Killigrew's Early Managerial Career: Carolean Stage Rivalry in London, 1663–1668'. *Restoration & Eighteenth-Century Theatre Research*, vol. 27, no. 2, 2012, pp. 13–33.

Moore, Robert E. 'The Music for *Macbeth*'. *The Musical Quarterly*, vol. 47, no. 1, 1961, pp. 22–40.

Murray, Barbara A. *Restoration Shakespeare: Viewing the Voice*. London: Associated University Presses, 2001.

Owen, Susan J. *Restoration Theatre and Crisis*. Oxford: Oxford University Press, 1996.

— *Perspectives on Restoration Drama*. Manchester: Manchester University Press, 2002.

Patterson, Annabel. *Censorship and Interpretation: The Conditions of Writing and Reading in Early Modern England*. Madison: The University of Wisconsin Press, 1984.

Payne, Deborah C. 'Reified Object or Emergent Professional? Retheorizing the Restoration Actress'. In *Cultural Readings of Restoration and Eighteenth-Century English Theatre*, edited by J. Douglas Canfield, and

Deborah C. Payne. Athens: The University of Georgia Press, 1995, pp. 13–38.

'"Damn You, Davenant!": The Perils and Possibilities of Restoration Shakespeare'. *Restoration & Eighteenth-Century Theatre Research*, vol. 32, no. 1, 2017, pp. 21–40.

The Business of English Restoration Theatre, 1660–1700. Cambridge: Cambridge University Press, 2024.

Payne Fisk, Deborah. 'The Restoration Actress'. In *A Companion to Restoration Drama*, edited by Susan J. Owen. Oxford: Blackwell, 2008, pp. 69–91.

Pepys, Samuel. *The Diary of Samuel Pepys*, edited by Robert Latham, and William Matthews. 11 vols. London: HarperCollins, 1995.

Plank, Steven E. '"And Now about the Cauldron Sing": Music and the Supernatural on the Restoration Stage'. *Early Music*, vol. 18, no. 3, 1990, pp. 392–407.

Prieto-Pablo, Juan A. 'Restoration Actors and Actresses and Their Acting Roles', Universidad de Sevilla. https://institucional.us.es/restoratio nactors/web/. Accessed 12 November 2024.

Reimers, Sara. 'Davenant's Lady Macduff and the Subversion of Normative Femininity in Twenty-First-Century Performance'. In *Performing Restoration Shakespeare*, edited by Amanda Eubanks Winkler, Claude Fretz, and Richard Schoch. Cambridge: Cambridge University Press, 2023, pp. 142–162.

Reimers, Sara, and Richard Schoch. 'Performing Restoration Shakespeare Today: Staging Davenant's *Macbeth*'. *Shakespeare Bulletin*, vol. 37, no. 4, 2019, pp. 467–489.

Ritchie, Fiona. 'Cross-Dressing in Restoration Shakespeare: *Twelfth Night* and *The Tempest*'. In *Performing Restoration Shakespeare*, edited by Amanda Eubanks Winkler, Claude Fretz, and Richard Schoch. Cambridge: Cambridge University Press, 2023, pp. 79–96.

Roberts, David. *Thomas Betterton: The Greatest Actor of the Restoration Stage*. Cambridge: Cambridge University Press, 2010.

'Thomas Killigrew, Theatre Manager'. In *Thomas Killigrew: Revisionary Essays*, edited by Philip Major. Farnham: Ashgate, 2013, pp. 63–90.

Robert David, and Richard Palmer. 'Harris vs Harris: A Restoration Actor at the Court of Arches'. *Huntington Library Quarterly*, forthcoming.

Rosenfeld, Sybil. 'Some Notes on the Players in Oxford, 1661–1713'. *Review of English Studies*, vol. 19, 1943, pp. 366–375.

Rosenthal, Laura J. *Playwrights and Plagiarists in Early Modern England: Gender, Authorship, Literary Property*. Ithaca, NY: Cornell University Press, 1996.

Rothstein, Eric. *Restoration Tragedy: Form and the Process of Change*. Madison: University of Wisconsin Press, 1967.

Rothstein, Eric, and Frances M. Kavenik. *The Designs of Carolean Comedy*. Carbondale: Southern Illinois University Press, 1988.

Rutter, Tom. *Shakespeare and the Admiral's Men: Reading across Repertories on the London Stage, 1594–1600*. Cambridge: Cambridge University Press, 2017.

Scheil, Katherine. *The Taste of the Town: Shakespearian Comedy and the Early Eighteenth-Century Theater*. Lewisburg: Bucknell University Press, 2003.

Schoch, Richard. *Writing the History of the British Stage, 1660–1900*. Cambridge: Cambridge University Press, 2016.

Shakespeare, William. *Mr. William Shakespeare's Comedies, Histories, & Tragedies*. London, 1623.

The Tragedy of Hamlet Prince of Denmark. London, 1676.

The Oxford Shakespeare: The Complete Works, edited by John Jowett, William Montgomery, Gary Taylor, and Stanley Wells. 2nd ed. Oxford: Oxford University Press, 2005.

Sorelius, Gunnar. *'The Giant Race before the Flood': Pre-Restoration Drama on the Stage and in the Criticism of the Restoration.* Uppsala: Almqvist 7 Wiksells, 1966.

'The Rights of the Restoration Theatrical Companies in the Older Drama'. *Studia Neophilologica*, vol. 37, 1965, no. 1, pp. 174–189.

Southern, Richard. *Changeable Scenery: Its Origin and Development in the British Theatre.* London: Faber & Faber, 1952.

Spencer, Christopher, ed. *Davenant's 'Macbeth' from the Yale Manuscript: An Edition, with a Discussion of the Relation of Davenant's Text to Shakespeare's.* New Haven, CT: Yale University Press, 1961.

'"Count Paris's Wife": *Romeo and Juliet* on the Early Restoration Stage'. *Texas Studies in Language and Literature*, vol. 7, 1965–66, pp. 309–316.

ed. *Five Restoration Adaptations of Shakespeare.* Urbana: University of Illinois, 1965.

'*Macbeth* and Davenant's *The Rivals*'. *Shakespeare Quarterly*, vol. 20, no. 2, 1969, pp. 225–229.

Spencer, Hazelton. *Shakespeare Improved: The Restoration Versions in Quarto and on the Stage.* Cambridge, MA: Harvard University Press, 1927.

Stapylton, Robert. *The Step-Mother.* London, 1664.

Stern, Tiffany. *Rehearsal from Shakespeare to Sheridan.* Oxford: Oxford University Press, 2000.

Summers, Montague, ed. *Shakespeare Adaptations: 'The Tempest', 'The Mock Tempest', and 'King Lear'.* London: Jonathan Cape, 1922.

Van Lennep, William, Emmett L. Avery, and Arthur H. Southen. *The London Stage, 1660–1800: Part 1, 1660–1700.* Carbondale and Edwardsville: Southern Illinois University Press, 1965. [*LS*]

Waith, Eugene M. *Ideas of Greatness: Heroic Drama in England.* London: Routledge & Paul Kegan, 1971.

Walden, Richard. *Io Ruminans: Or the Repercussion of a Triumph Celebrated in the Palace of Diana Adenna*. London, 1662.

Walkling, Andrew R. *Masque and Opera in England, 1656–1688*. Abingdon: Routledge, 2017.

English Dramatick Opera, 1661–1706. Abingdon: Routledge, 2019.

Watkins, Stephen. 'Competing Heroes? Genre, Repertory, and Rivalry on the Early Restoration Stage'. In *Restoration Reshaping: Shifting Forms, Genres and Conventions in English Theatre, 1660–1737*, edited by Anna Mikyskova, and Filip Krajnik. Prague: Charles University Karolinum Press, forthcoming.

'The Protectorate Playhouse: William Davenant's Cockpit in the 1650s'. *Shakespeare Bulletin*, vol. 37, no. 1, 2019, pp. 89–109.

'Dryden, Shakespeare, and Learning the Trade: "I Have Profess'd to Imitate the Divine *Shakespeare*"'. In *Shakespeare, Education and Pedagogy: Representations, Interactions and Adaptations*, edited by Pamela Bickley, and Jenny Stevens. London: Routledge, 2023, pp. 15–22. [Watkins 2023a]

'Heroic Shakespeare at Lincoln's Inn Fields'. In *Performing Restoration Shakespeare*, edited by Amanda Eubanks Winkler, Claude Fretz, and Richard Schoch. Cambridge: Cambridge University Press, 2023, pp. 38–60. [Watkins 2023b]

Wikander, Matthew H. '"The Duke My Father's Wrack": The Innocence of the Restoration *Tempest*'. *Shakespeare Survey*, vol. 43, 1991, pp. 91–98.

Wilson, John Harold. *All the King's Ladies: Actresses of the Restoration*. Chicago, IL: University of Chicago Press, 1958.

Winn, James A. *John Dryden and His World*. New Haven, CT: Yale University Press, 1987.

'Dryden's Songs'. In *Enchanted Ground: Reimagining John Dryden*, edited by Jayne Lewis, and Maximilian E. Novak. Toronto: Toronto University Press, 2004, pp. 290–317.

Wood, Anthony. *The Life and Times of Anthony Wood, Antiquary, of Oxford, 1632–1695, Described by Himself: Volume I: 1632–1663*, edited by Andrew Clark. Oxford: Clarendon Press, 1891.

Acknowledgements

All figures are reproduced courtesy of the Folger Shakespeare Library, Washington, DC, under a Creative Commons Attribution-ShareAlike 4.0 International License.

I am grateful to the series Editor, W. B. Worthen, for his support for and advice on this project, as well as to the two anonymous readers for their suggestions for improvements, many of which I have adopted.

My thanks also to Krithika Shivakumar for their patience and care during the copyediting and production process.

The Element is dedicated to Sarah Smyth, with love.

Cambridge Elements ⸗

Shakespeare Performance

W. B. Worthen
Barnard College

W. B. Worthen is Alice Brady Pels Professor in the Arts, and Chair of the Theatre Department at Barnard College. He is also co-chair of the Ph.D. Program in Theatre at Columbia University, where he is Professor of English and Comparative Literature.

ADVISORY BOARD

Pascale Aebischer, University of Exeter
Todd Landon Barnes, Ramapo College of New Jersey
Susan Bennett, University of Calgary
Rustom Bharucha, Jawaharlal Nehru University, New Delhi
Gina Bloom, University of California, Davis
Bridget Escolme, Queen Mary University of London
Alan Galey, University of Toronto
Douglas Lanier, University of New Hampshire
Julia Reinhard Lupton, University of California, Irvine
Peter W. Marx, University of Köln
Sonia Massai, King's College London
Alfredo Michel Modenessi, National Autonomous University of Mexico
Robert Shaughnessy, Guildford School of Acting, University of Surrey
Ayanna Thompson, George Washington University
Yong Li-Lan, National University of Singapore

About the Series

Shakespeare Performance is a dynamic collection in a field that is both always emerging and always evanescent. Responding to the global range of Shakespeare performance today, the series launches provocative, urgent criticism for researchers, graduate students and practitioners. Publishing scholarship with a direct bearing on the contemporary contexts of Shakespeare performance, it considers specific performances, material and social practices, ideological and cultural frameworks, emerging and significant artists and performance histories.

Cambridge Elements⁼

Shakespeare Performance

ELEMENTS IN THE SERIES

A Short History of Shakespeare in Performance: From the Restoration to the Twenty–First Century
Richard Schoch

Viral Shakespeare: Performance in the Time of Pandemic
Pascale Aebischer

This Distracted Globe: Attending to Distraction in Shakespeare's Theatre
Jennifer J. Edwards

Shakespeare without Print
Paul Menzer

Shakespeare's Visionary Women
Laura Jayne Wright

Early Modern Media Ecology
Peter W. Marx

Sleep No More and the Discourses of Shakespeare Performance
D. J. Hopkins

Staging Disgust: Rape, Shame, and Performance in Shakespeare and Middleton
Jennifer Panek

Extended Reality Shakespeare
Aneta Mancewicz

Approaching the Interval in the Early Modern Theatre: The Significance of the 'Act-Time'
Mark Hutchings

Shakespeare and Nonhuman Intelligence
Heather Warren-Crow

Shakespeare and the Restoration Repertory
Stephen Watkins

A full series listing is available at: www.cambridge.org/ESPF